A FIRE FALLS

Moving Into Holy Spirit Fire

John answered, saying to all, "I indeed baptize you with water; but One mightier than I is coming, whose sandal strap I am not worthy to loose. He will baptize you with the Holy Spirit and fire."
(Luke 3:16)

JAMES A. DURHAM

TABLE OF CONTENTS

ACKNOWLEDGEMENTS

This book came as a gift from the Lord. Therefore, I want to express my thanks first and foremost to Him for providing the revelation for this book and for inspiration along the way to complete the work. This book has been five years in the making and the Lord had to prod me several times to get it completed. I am grateful for the loving push I received from Him. The Lord is good and His love and mercy endure forever.

I want to acknowledge the invaluable assistance I received from my extremely blessed, highly favored, and anointed wife, Gloria. I am grateful for her dedicated and tireless assistance in proof reading the book and confirming the accuracy of the scriptural references. I also want to acknowledge my daughter, Michelle, who remains a constant and consistent cheerleader throughout the process of all my writings. In the last several months, Michelle has asked almost daily about my progress on the book. I am so thankful to the Lord that He placed both of these two amazing women in my life and constantly blesses me through their love and support!

PREFACE

After completing the first draft of this book, I went through it again to wordsmith the contents for clarity and to correct typographical errors. Then I put it down as we departed on a ministry trip to the United Kingdom (UK). At the invitation of our spiritual daughter and ministry board member, MiSo Yun, her mother and her son we were going to the UK on a sightseeing tour and to provide ministry in three churches in London. During our time there, we traveled to Wales for three days and two nights. Our goal was to visit the hometown and home church of Evan Roberts, the revivalist in the 1904-1905 Welsh Revival. We had reservations to stay in a Bed and Breakfast Inn called Island House. It was formerly the home of Evan Roberts.

Before we departed on this adventure, I had a strong and compelling vision from the Lord. I saw an old fireplace with piles of ashes at the bottom. It looked as if the flame had gone out long ago and the fire had grown completely cold over time. As I stood looking at the ashes, the Lord handed me a staff about three and a half feet long, and pointed toward the fireplace. I put one end of the staff into the ashes and began to gently stir them around to see what was under the surface. Before long I found a live coal and began to joyously blow on it and bring it back to a flame. I added more wood as I continued to fan the flames and finally got a blazing fire going. I felt certain that this was a prophetic word about something we would see on our trip to the UK. I thought about what Paul said in 2 Timothy 1:6 (NIV), "*For this reason I remind you to fan into flame the gift of God, which is in you through the laying on of my hands.*"

As we travelled to Wales, I expected to see a fireplace somewhere and to release a prophetic word about fanning the flames and getting the fires of revival going again. In the Island house, I found that the fireplaces had been replaced by devices with artificial flames. There were no ashes. As we toured the Moriah School Room and the Moriah Chapel, I did not see a fireplace. However I was still hoping that I would see something of this vision manifest on our visit to the land of revival. I thought about 1 Kings 18:38-39, "*Then the fire of the Lord fell and consumed the burnt sacrifice, and the wood and the stones and the dust, and it licked up the water that was in the trench. Now when all the people saw it, they fell on their faces; and they said, 'The Lord, He is God! The Lord, He is God!'*" I want to see the fire of God fall once more with such power that it will turn the hearts of everyone back to true faith and allegiance to our Father God.

During our visit to Wales, we were very blessed to get a briefing on the Welsh Revival of 1904-1905 and the life of Evan Roberts by Alun Ebenezer and his wife Pearl. As a boy, Alun knew Evan Roberts personally. He was a family friend and often visited in his family's home. It was such an unexpected privilege to hear about the man and the revival from someone who actually knew Evan Roberts. It had long been my dream to visit these places and I expressed that to Alun after he shared the story with us. We began to talk and our thirty minute invitation turned into a two hour visit. While my wife and our friends sang old hymns played on the piano by Pearl, Alun and I continued to visit about the great things the Lord had done in Wales.

After several minutes, I shared with Alun my vision, but expressed some disappointment that I had not seen the fireplace. Suddenly his eyes lit up and he became very excited about this vision. Then he said: "Would you like to see the fireplace? There is only one left. All the others have been sealed up and covered over to keep the heat in." He escorted me to the Moriah School Room next to the chapel and led me to a back room where children and young people had received training during the revival. Evan Roberts had taught in this room many times. To my great joy, I saw the fireplace. We began to pray and make decrees for the fires of revival to fall on Wales once more. I prayed for revival fires to fall on South Korea and America as well. Alun said that he was excited to tell some of the other intercessors about the vision and our experience at the fireplace.

Something unusual happened in the school room, the chapel, and the cemetery. None of my pictures were clear. In each picture, it appeared that a cloud of light was present between the camera and the objects I was trying to photograph. On the top left side of the fireplace stood a picture of Evan Roberts. The picture was covered with much more light than the rest of the fireplace. At first, I thought this had something to do with light coming through the windows. I soon learned that it was in the pictures from every angle and almost every part of these places we were visiting. I could not avoid the appearance of the light. It seemed to be the glory light of the Lord still manifesting in these special places. Then I was struck by how appropriate the vision and our experiences were to the message of this book, and decided to include them as a way of sharing the light and fire of God with you.

Back in Moriah Chapel, I felt myself drawn to one particular pew near the chancel area and just behind the bench for the pianist. As I sat in this seat, I felt led to lean on the back of the pew in front of me and put my head on the wooden surface as I prayed. Then I felt compelled to put my hands and head over the pew. As I did this, I felt something of the Spirit of God falling on me. I glanced to the left and saw a column of light shining down from the ceiling over the balcony and touching the left side of my body and face. There was no window or opening in this part of the sealing. The light was something spiritual and supernatural. Something which felt like electricity began to flow through my body from this unusual column of light. So, I sat as long as I could soaking in the presence of the Lord. This energy continued to flow through my body as long as we stayed in the chapel. It was like an electrical current continuously flowing through me. I felt it over and over as I moved from place to place in both buildings. It was especially strong in certain spots and I came to believe that these were the exact places where the Lord had manifested powerfully during the revival of 1904-1905.

I was unaware of what this experience truly meant until I returned home and watched a video about the revival. I had ordered it while we were in the UK and it arrived the day after we returned home. As I watched the video, I was very pleasantly surprised to see that the actor portraying Evan Roberts was shown three times sitting in the exact spot where I sat in Moriah Chapel. I also saw a portrayal of his experience of the baptism of the Holy Spirit which he experienced in a different chapel. In the video, he sat with his head over the pew and with his arms hanging over the pew screen in front of him. This is exactly what I had been led to do before the column of light came over me. This positioning of my arms over the pew was how Evan had been positioned when he finally received an answer to long months of prayer to be baptized in the Holy Spirit. I have dreamed about this experience over and over since our return, and it feels as if that anointing from the Lord continues to grow stronger with time.

As we left the chapel, Alun and Pearl came out with us and we took their picture. This time the picture was perfectly clear. Alun then made a suggestion for us to visit the river just a short distance from the home of Evan Roberts at 8:00 p.m. when high tide was predicted to come in. He spoke of the revival being at low tide now, but that just as the water comes back in from the ocean tides revival will return. Then he suggested that we go back at 8:00 a.m. to see the low tide. We decided to make these two visits to the river, and I am so happy that we did. We discussed in our group the prophetic significance of the number eight and began to decree new beginnings for the fires of revival in Wales, South Korea and the USA.

We decided to walk to the river at 7:30 p.m. and we are happy that we did this. The tide was already coming in and we would have missed much of the glory if we had waited. As the tide came in, the sun was setting on the opposite side of the river. As it grew close to the horizon, the color changed to a very bright orange and it appeared to be ablaze. Then the reflection of the setting sun began to move across the water and it seemed that the water itself was on fire. The lower the sun's position, the wider its image on the surface of the water. This seemed to be a powerful prophetic word about this spiritual season and an imminent reappearance of the revival fires. I received this as another prophetic word about our own spiritual journey. The closer we get to the Son, the more clearly we will see and receive more of the glory of God.

Suddenly, we heard a series of explosions near a farmhouse across the river, and flames began to leap into the air. There were a total of three explosions as we watched a fire break out in the natural. We understood these three explosions to be a prophetic promise for a manifestation of the Father, the Son, and the Holy Spirit when the revival fires break out again. At this point, it began to look like this prophetic word about revival fires was shifting from the spiritual realm to the natural. I feel and believe that the time is so close at hand. The fire continued to burn for several minutes and was still blazing as we made our way back in the dark to our room in Evan Roberts' house.

As we went to bed, I began to feel a very strong sense of burning on my entire face. My wife asked if I was okay because my face had suddenly appeared to be very red. I assured her that I was okay. Then I started to soak in the fire of God as we attempted to sleep in Evan's old bedroom. The presence of the Lord was too strong on both nights for us to actually sleep well in that place. Being unable to sleep deeply was not a problem for us. We received it as a blessing from the Lord. This was not the only time I felt a strong sense of fire on my face. It came again on another night before we returned home from this trip, and it has manifested twice since we returned home. May the Lord set your face and heart on fire once again to prepare you for what is coming next!

We rose early the next morning in order to visit the river at 8:00 a.m. to see the low tide. To our surprise the tide was already coming back in. We arrived in time to see some of the things which emerged with the low tide, but it didn't last long. Seagulls were harvesting food on the islands which emerged with the low tide. A fisherman had been out casting a line in the water to harvest a fresh meal. This too seemed like a prophetic word from the Lord. The tides are coming in before they are expected and the season of revival is close at hand. I believe that many will be surprised to see it emerge before expected. Others will be up early to position themselves to be fed by the emergence of the Lord's planned provision for a new wave of revival.

The high tide had revealed images of fire and glory coming from the heavens and blazing on the earth. On the other hand, the low tide revealed something very different. We saw the mud, the floating debris, and the predators which came out to pray on the stranded, the vulnerable, and the weak. It seemed as if the low tide revealed all the filthy and base things in nature and in most living beings. This seemed to be another powerful prophetic word about revival. It pointed to our great need for a rising tide to return the things of God and reflect His glory again. We need a cleansing flow of living water to wash us and make us new. We need the covering which heals, protects, and lifts us to a higher level. I continue to meditate on it every day and dream about it every night. It is the central focus in my prayers and meditations. Even so, come quickly Lord Jesus! Amen and Amen!

While we were in Wales, I ordered several books on the revival written by eyewitnesses. These arrived with the video on the day after our return. As I began to read these books, I was surprised to see how often they referred to the revival in terms of high tides and low tides. They also spoke of the river as prophetic of the return of revival to the land. I noted how often they spoke of the fire falling on individuals and groups in the same places where we experienced these gifts from the Lord. It was also noted that Evan Roberts often felt the presence of the Lord as being like an electrical current flowing through his body. When he felt this powerful presence of the Lord, he would rise up to speak in the meetings.

We are more and more grateful to the Lord for demonstrating the same phenomena to us which were experienced by people in the revival. He was releasing these same spiritual gifts in our own time of visitation in these places. The Lord is good and His mercy endures forever. Many have said that the revival began with tears, continued with tears and ended when the tears stopped flowing. Repentance is at the heart of every true revival. I am reminded of the teaching in James 4:8-10, *"Draw near to God and He will draw near to you. Cleanse your hands, you sinners; and purify your hearts, you double-minded. Lament and mourn and weep! Let your laughter be turned to mourning and your joy to gloom. Humble yourselves in the sight of the Lord, and He will lift you up."* This seems to be a very accurate description of the stages of the revival in Wales. Perhaps these words from the book of James are the key to the return of revival fires in our time.

I am still heavily influenced by what we experienced in Wales as we attempted to sleep two nights in Evan Roberts' former bedroom; had breakfast in the dining room where he ate his meals and taught small groups; visited Pisgah Chapel where he taught students; spent time in Moriah Chapel and Moriah School Room where revival broke out, and as we stood in the Moriah Cemetery looking down on the spot where Evan Roberts was buried with his family. Over and over, we encountered the presence of the living Lord and the Holy Spirit as well as angels from the realms of glory. It seems as if part of my spirit was left there and a part of his spirit came back with us. I think about it while awake and dream about it at night. I sense that the Lord is about to lead us into another great awakening of the

Holy Spirit and will soon release fresh revival fires. I am sincerely praying for it! How about you?

In the days following these powerful experiences in Wales, I continue to study the origins and messages of the great revival which broke out in 1904. As I read, meditate, dream and process these things, I am more and more convinced that we need to get back to the centrality of Jesus Christ in all we do. I want to proclaim with the Apostle Paul, "*For I determined not to know anything among you except Jesus Christ and Him crucified.*" (1 Corinthians 2:2) In this season as we prepare for revival and a great harvest, we must get focused back on the cross of Calvary and turn our hearts to the Savior who paid such an aweful price for our restoration with His precious blood. On that cross He removed everything which hinders our walk with Him. All we have to do is extend our hands and receive it by faith. I urge you to do this right now. To fully receive the things released in this book, you need to be born again and Spirit filled. The Lord is willing and you only have to ask.

Spirit filled men and women must kneel in prayer and then rise again with new power to reach the world for Yeshua ha Messiach. Time is short and the call is clear. Now is the day of salvation and none of us can afford to miss the hour of our visitation! I am crying out again, "More fire Lord! More fire! It hurts so good!" We need to be cleansed by His flames and fired up for what the Lord is releasing right now. May we have flames on our heads and Holy Spirit fire in our hearts!

PRAYERS

I am praying that you will experience a fire falling on you as you read the words of this testimony and as you go through the following chapters of this book. I am praying that the presence of the Holy Spirit will pulse through your body like a field of electricity and that you will feel the powerful presence of the Lord with you. I am praying for your face and your heart to burn with the fire of God. May the light from heaven shine on you and release a fresh anointing to prepare you for a season of great harvest for the Kingdom of God. I am praying all these things in faith and in the mighty name of Yeshua ha Messiach. Amen and Amen!

> *Return, we beseech You, O God of hosts; look down from heaven and see, and visit this vine and the vineyard which Your right hand has planted, and the branch that You made strong for Yourself. It is burned with fire, it is cut down; they perish at the rebuke of Your countenance. Let Your hand be upon the man of Your right hand, upon the son of man whom You made strong for Yourself. Then we will not turn back from You; revive us, and we will call upon Your name. Restore us, O LORD God of hosts; cause Your face to shine, and we shall be saved!* (Psalm 80:14-19)

> *Will You not revive us again, that Your people may rejoice in You? Show us Your mercy, LORD, and grant us Your salvation.* (Psalm 85:6-7)

INTRODUCTION

Vision Report
Thursday, Feb 19, 2015

This morning the Presence of the Lord was very strong. I went into His Presence with a clear purpose this morning. While I prayed, I was given a vision of an opening in Heaven at a short distance ahead. As I watched, however, it seemed to be getting further away instead of closer. Clouds began to close in so that I could no longer see the open portal. I made several decrees against all forms of deception which attempt to cloud our ability to see and experience the Open Heaven. Then I looked behind and saw that I was still ascending toward Heaven at a very fast rate of speed. It seemed odd that Heaven seemed both closer and further away at the same time.

Then I heard the Lord say, "A Changing of the Guard!" My thoughts went to the passing of several of the key leaders and spiritual generals recently. I didn't perceive that there was anything negative about their departure. They were going to a great reward in Heaven. At the same time, it is time for a changing of the guard, because the Lord is doing a new thing. In this season, it is necessary for new people to come forward to accomplish this purpose for the Lord. We need to be open for more changes of the guard. It has only begun. More will follow. We must cope with the understanding that this is not a loss or penalty for these spiritual giants, but a promotion. This move of the Lord is opening the door for an acceleration of the things these individuals labored in the heat of the day to establish.

I started to cry out for a fresh anointing of fire from the Holy Spirit. I began to cry out for a fresh baptism of fire for all of those moving in the Spirit in this season. Suddenly, I saw an amazing sight. It looked like a waterfall, but it was fire coming down from the Open Heaven. Then I understood this is why I did not go up through the portal. It was because the portal was for an outpouring. The word which came into my mind evolved from waterfall, to Fire Fall, and then to "Firefall." We need to get under the "Firefall" of the Lord so that we can be re-fired for the work of the Kingdom in this season. I moved toward this outpouring and prayed for the Lord to remove everything that hinders us from moving with Him in this season. Are we ready for it? I think the answer is, "No!" This is why we need the fresh anointing of fire promised in the Gospel of the Kingdom. I am seeking it with all my heart. How about you?

Earlier, I had been interceding for a great evangelistic outpouring in Israel. I was praying for 1,000 unsaved Jewish people to accept Yeshua ha Messiach. As I prayed for this to manifest, I heard the Lord say, "Why not 2,000?" So, I started to pray for the 2,000 when I heard the Lord say, "Why not 3,000? It is time for another outpouring like the disciples saw on the Day of Pentecost." I believe this is a season to increase our expectations and get focused on a great end-time harvest. I believe the magnitude of this harvest will be a surprise even for those who think they are already expecting enough. The Lord always gives more than we ask or think. So, let's ask and think for lots more! Amen?

(End of Vision Report)
EXTENDING YOUR TENT PEGS

As we prepared for a ministry trip to Korea, we visited a church conference. The worship leader cried out, "Stretch out your tent pegs! Increase your capacity to receive!" Something about those words really resonated with me. On that ministry trip, I asked people at each church we visited, "Do you want to receive more?" Then I challenged them to extend their own tent pegs. This was the Lord's challenge to Israel in the days of Isaiah. He continues to extend this challenge to us through the words of the prophet.

> *Clear lots of ground for your tents! Make your tents large. Spread out! Think big! Use plenty of rope, drive the tent pegs deep. You're going to need lots of elbow room for your growing family. You're going to take over whole nations; you're going to resettle abandoned cities.* (Isaiah 54:2-3, TMSG)

I pray that you are also hearing and feeling this challenge. Do you want to receive more? Most of us cry out for more. We seek the double portion outpouring as well as the hundredfold increase on the seeds we sow into the Kingdom. If you are seeking increase, then get into position to receive it. It is time to extend the tent pegs of your faith. Perhaps you are wondering how to do that. It is so simple. All you have to do is ask. Remember Jesus' words in Matthew 7:7-8, "*Ask, and it will be given to you; seek, and you will find; knock, and it will be opened to you.*

For everyone who asks receives, and he who seeks finds, and to him who knocks it will be opened."

The words of Jesus are consistent with the work of the Lord throughout history as reported in the Bible. Do you remember the prayer of Jabez? He boldly asked the Lord for more and the Lord answered that prayer by granting his request. Now is the time for boldness. This is the season to press in for more. For a long time, I prayed this prayer several times every day. As with Jabez, the Lord answered and I received. Perhaps this is a good time for you to begin praying this simple prayer daily:

> *Now Jabez was more honorable than his brothers, and his mother called his name Jabez, saying, "Because I bore him in pain." And Jabez called on the God of Israel saying, "Oh, that You would bless me indeed, and enlarge my territory, that Your hand would be with me, and that You would keep me from evil, that I may not cause pain!" So God granted him what he requested."* (1 Chronicles 4:9-10)

ASK AND YOU SHALL RECEIVE!

If you want Jabez sized results, pray Jabez sized prayers. It is a promise of Jesus! Do you believe Him? I think this is one of the major blockages in the church. People believe Jesus said these things, but they don't really believe that it is for them. They look at these passages in the Bible and only see them as historical messages for a previous time and an ancient people. I have a different attitude about the Word of God. I believe that every promise in the Bible is for me. These promises are also for you. I challenge you to study the promise of Jesus in Luke, Chapter Eleven and claim it for yourself.

> *So I say to you, ask, and it will be given to you; seek, and you will find; knock, and it will be opened to you. For everyone who asks receives, and he who seeks finds, and to him who knocks it will be opened. If a son asks for bread from any father among you, will he give him a stone? Or if he asks for a fish, will he give him a serpent instead of a fish? Or if he asks for an egg, will he offer him a scorpion? If you then, being evil, know how to give good gifts to your children, how much more will your heavenly Father give the Holy Spirit to those who ask Him*! (Luke 11:9-13)

Think about it! If you know how to bless your children, how much more is Father God willing to bless you? This is why we need to clearly see that we are the children of God. He is a good Father. He is the best of all fathers. There is no one running a close second. He is good all the time, and He wants to be good to you right now. Are you ready to receive it? Then build up your faith and ask, but remember that you must ask believing His Word. In other words, you need to put your faith behind your prayers.

In this passage from Luke, notice that Jesus tied this promise to the giving of the Holy Spirit. It is clear from Jesus' teaching that we are to ask for the Father to give us the Holy Spirit. We do this trusting that He will do it. "*For the LORD is good; His mercy is everlasting, and His truth endures to all generations.*" (Psalm 100:5) As promised, we can trust Him because He is good and His love and mercy endure forever. We can always ask for more. This kind of prayer has His blessing and His anointing. It is time to get busy praying for increase more and more. Amen?

Now let's take this one step further. Remember the promise made by John the Baptizer in Luke 3:16. "*John answered, saying to all, 'I indeed baptize you with water; but One mightier than I is coming, whose sandal strap I am not worthy to loose. He will baptize you with the Holy Spirit and fire.'*" If we can believe Jesus' promise to give us the Holy Spirit, can't we take it a step further and include the promised fire. Think about it. If you want more Holy Spirit fire, all you have to do is ask. I don't know about you, but I always want more. So, I am constantly praying for more Holy Spirit fire and a greater impartation of the Holy Spirit baptism. One of my regular and favorite prayers is: "More fire Lord. More fire. It hurts so good."

We minister often in South Korea. Last year we were there three different times for a total of almost three months. We had the great joy of serving in many different churches throughout the nation. One of the things we have noticed is that Korean people press in for the things of God more than most others. They are hungry and they are desperate to receive more of the Bread of Heaven. They know their thirst and they are boldly pressing in to drink more from the flow of living waters. Do you believe that it is good to press in for more of the things of the Spirit? If you do, it is time to get moving and press in daily for more fire.

Jesus seemed to support this idea as He promised that when we ask we will receive, when we seek we will find and when we knock it will be opened for us. If you agree, I challenge you to be bold and seek more. If you believe that it is good to be bold and ask, then press in right now to receive it. Whatever you have received in the past, this is the time to stir it up. Remember how Paul advised Timothy in 2 Timothy 1:6, "*I remind you to stir up the gift of God which is in you through the laying on of my hands.*" I like the way it is translated in the NIV, "*I remind you to fan into flame the gift of God*" After all, we are talking about the fire of God which comes with the baptism of the Holy Spirit. If your fire is almost out, stir up the ashes and find a live coal. Then fan it into a flame as you put more of the fuel of faith on the fire.

BELIEVE YOU CAN RECEIVE

If you want the gift of fire, it is critically important for you to believe that you can receive it. If you have the fire but you want more, keep pressing in for it and fanning it into a flame. Jesus repeatedly told people that they would receive what they expected or what they believed. It is time to raise the bar of faith up another notch or two. Build up your faith. I remind you of the advice given in Jude 1:20-21, "*But you, beloved, building yourselves up on your most holy faith, praying in the Holy Spirit, keep yourselves in the love of God, looking for the mercy of our Lord Jesus Christ unto eternal life.*"

Many people are sitting around waiting for someone else to give it to them. Some are seeking an anointed person to impart these gifts. That is okay. It May be that this is the Lord's plan for you, however, I recommend that you take action on your own part. Remember: "*And the spirits of the prophets are subject to the prophets.*" (1 Corinthians 14:32) Your spirit is subject to you. Begin to take authority over your own spirit and get it moving in the right direction. Think about what James is teaching in the passage below as he sheds light on what we can expect when we ask:

> *If any of you lacks wisdom, he should ask*
> *God, who gives generously to all without*

finding fault, and it will be given to him. But when he asks, he must believe and not doubt, because he who doubts is like a wave of the sea, blown and tossed by the wind. That man should not think he will receive anything from the Lord; he is a double–minded man, unstable in all he does. (James 1:5-8, NIV)

Obviously, this promise is specifically talking about asking for wisdom. I am convinced that we all need more wisdom, and it is good to keep asking for it. I also believe that we can expand on this teaching to include asking for Holy Spirit Fire. Many people do not have fire because they haven't asked for it. Remember what James taught in James 4:2b-3, "*Yet you do not have because you do not ask. You ask and do not receive, because you ask amiss, that you may spend it on your pleasures.*" If you are asking to be empowered to do the work of the Kingdom you are not asking amiss. At the same time, you need to understand that asking is a critical step in being ready to receive. Remember, you must believe that you will receive when you ask. Don't let doubt rob you of the fire of God! Amen?

THERE IS MORE TO THE PROMISE

Submit yourselves, then, to God. Resist the devil, and he will flee from you. Come near to God and he will come near to you. Wash your hands, you sinners, and purify your hearts, you double–minded. Grieve, mourn and wail. Change your laughter to mourning and your joy to gloom. Humble yourselves before the Lord, and he will lift you up. (James 4:7-10, NIV)

Think about it! You can be healed of double-mindedness. If you struggle to believe these promises are for you, that is the essence of double-mindedness. But there is good news. This is not a permanent condition. There are steps you can take to be healed of this spiritual ailment. Follow James' advice: Humble yourself before the Lord and let Him lift you up. Submit to Him and be set free from all demonic oppression. Wash your hands and purify your heart so that you can ascend God's holy hill. Jesus has done it all for you. I encourage you to receive by faith all that He won for you on the cross of Calvary! Amen? My continuous prayer is, "More fire Lord! More fire! It hurts so good!"

PRAYER

"Adonai said to Moshe, 'Speak to Aharon and his sons, and tell them that this is how you are to bless the people of Isra'el: you are to say to them,

'Y'varekh'kha Adonai v'yishmerekha,
[May Adonai bless you and keep you.]

Ya'er Adonai panav eleikha vichunekka.
[May Adonai make his face shine on you and show you his favor.]

Yissa Adonai panav eleikha v'yasem l'kha shalom.
[May Adonai lift up his face toward you and give you peace.]'"

"In this way they are to put my name on the people of Isra'el, so that I will bless them." (Numbers 6:22-27, CJB)

CHAPTER ONE

FIRE AND PRAYER

And it came to pass, at the time of the offering of the evening sacrifice, that Elijah the prophet came near and said, "LORD God of Abraham, Isaac, and Israel, let it be known this day that You are God in Israel and I am Your servant, and that I have done all these things at Your word. Hear me, O LORD, hear me, that this people may know that You are the LORD God, and that You have turned their hearts back to You again." Then the fire of the LORD fell and consumed the burnt sacrifice, and the wood and the stones and the dust, and it licked up the water that was in the trench. Now when all the people saw it, they fell on their faces; and they said, "The LORD, He is God! The LORD, He is God!" (1 Kings 18:36-39)

Revival Fire Vision Report

While I lay face down on the floor at our Tuesday night soaking service, I went into an open vision in which I was lifted by the Spirit high above South Korea.

I was shown something similar to a view from a satellite. As I looked down on the Korean peninsula, I saw two powerful spiritual forces at war. I watched as a huge battle broke out between the powers of light and the powers of darkness. The Lord told me that South Korea is a vital link in the release of the end time harvest. Because the Korean people are so hungry for the Lord and so willing to press in to receive every anointing and every impartation, God will honor that hunger by releasing a massive revival that will spread around the world. When the Lord's plan was revealed, the enemy responded with a massive attack on the church in Korea attempting to rob this nation of its spiritual destiny and to delay the end time harvest.

I was reminded by the Lord of the many people we have met from South Korea in the last few months who have shared great spiritual struggles going on at this time in many of their churches. We have talked to some since their return to Korea who have experienced stronger warfare than ever in the church. The enemy is seeking those who are spiritually weak to use them to bring rebellion and disharmony to the body of Christ. These individuals are for the most part unaware that they are being influenced by the enemy to block the body of Christ in Korea and prevent the church from reaching its God-given destiny. I hear of people who are openly criticizing and attacking their pastors and their pastors' wives. These behaviors are bringing disunity to the body of Christ and causing great struggles within their congregations.

As this was being revealed to me, I saw angels kneeling and praying above Korea. I heard a call for Korean believers around the world to join together in agreement to break the power of darkness and to block the enemy's attempts to stop the great body of faith which God has called forth. I heard a call for people who are willing to forgo their limited desires for their own congregations and join together to pray for the kingdom of God to come on earth as it is in heaven. I heard a call for those who could fully support the advancement of the kingdom of God even if it didn't happen in their own churches. It is a call for people who are more kingdom focused than self-centered. It is for people who can rejoice when the church across the street grows faster than their own church. These are people who celebrate the advancement of the kingdom of God wherever it happens.

I heard a call for a people who could envision greater things for the nations; who can now think beyond anything they have ever imagined in the past. I heard the Lord calling for intercessors (prayer warriors) who are going after the nations because it is God's heart to win them all. I saw a huge circle of fire forming over Korea as God began to release this great revival. Shafts of light and fire were shooting forth from this circle and touching Korean people everywhere with the fire of revival. Korean people who have immigrated to various nations of the world were kindling the fire from Korea in other nations.

I shared with a group of pastors and church leaders what we had experienced at a church in Columbia, South Carolina a few weeks ago. The pastor asked the congregation, "How many churches are there in Columbia?" I wondered if they really knew because there are so many. The whole congregation answered correctly with one voice, as they shouted together: "One!" The pastor affirmed that their answer was correct. Jesus only has one church and we should be more concerned and committed to that church than our own small part in it. Wow! What insight! He has been teaching that for the last ten years, and they have all grasped this truth. I was thankful for this experience, because it widened my perspective.

The Lord called me to anoint those Korean pastors and leaders present in the meeting and to commission them for this awesome calling. The Holy Spirit was powerfully present with us as we participated in this commissioning service. I felt the fire of the Holy Spirit all through this conference. Others told me that they had also felt the fire of God. Are you feeling the fire now? It is time for the body of Christ to get fired up about the end-time harvest. It is time for us to get the fire and the zeal of the Holy Spirit to win the lost and build up the Kingdom of God on the Earth. It is time for us to get serious about obeying Jesus' commands which we call the "Great Commission." Are you ready for some fire?

The next morning the Lord placed it on my heart to share this vision and call on all His people to receive this commissioning and begin to be coals of fire around the world to ignite revival in all nations. Are you one of the ones willing to be a coal of fire for revival where God has placed you? If so, ask the Holy Spirit to release that anointing to you and join with us in a commitment to daily intercessory prayer for the release of God's power over your region, your nation and especially over the nation of South Korea. What starts there will go around the world into every nation on earth. Even now, the fires are beginning to break out. Thanks be to our God and Father! Thanks be to our Lord Jesus Christ who made it all possible! Thanks be to the Holy Spirit who carries the fire and releases it through us. Remember the words of the Lord in Zechariah 4:6b, "*Not by might nor by power, but by My Spirit,*" *says the Lord of hosts.*

(End of Vision Report)
SCRIPTURE RESEARCH

I have developed a pattern for study when the Lord gives me an assignment to prepare lessons or to write a book. In order to get an understanding of the importance of the topic, I compare it with another topic which is widely known to be very important in our walk of faith. One of the useful methods I have discovered is to consider the number of scriptural references to a particular topic and then compare that to the number of references about prayer. Most believers will readily admit that prayer is very important for every believer. If the topic I am researching has more references in the Bible than prayer, I believe it is very important to the Lord.

As I began researching the scriptures on the subject of fire, I found some interesting things. Fire is mentioned in the New King James Version (NKJV) of the Bible 503 times. In the New International Version (NIV) it is mentioned 423 times. In the King James Version (KJV) it is mentioned 506 times. I compared this with the number of times the word prayer is used in these translations. The results for comparison are: prayer is mentioned 106 times in the NKJV, 129 times in the NIV, and 109 times in the KJV. I thought about the sermons I had heard and preached in my lifetime. There were so many on prayer and yet so few on the fire of God. My conclusion is that fire is much more important to the Lord than it has been to us in the past.

FIRE IN RELATIONSHIPS

Most of the Biblical references to fire relate directly to our relationship with the Lord. He gives fire power to the prophetic words of His prophets. Think about what the Lord was saying in Jeremiah 23:29 (NIV), "*Is not my word like fire, declares the Lord, and like a hammer that breaks a rock in pieces*?" He starts fires on both the physical altars of the Tabernacle and Temple as well as in the temple of our hearts. He uses fire to cleanse, to purge, and to purify. He also uses it to destroy that which is unclean or impure. In the passages in each of the sections below, consider some of the ways the Lord uses fire in His relationships with His people.

FIRE PURIFIES LIPS

So I said: "Woe is me, for I am undone! Because I am a man of unclean lips, and I dwell in the midst of a people of unclean lips; for my eyes have seen the King, the Lord of hosts." Then one of the seraphim flew to me, having in his hand a live coal which he had taken with the tongs from the altar. And he touched my mouth with it, and said: "Behold, this has touched your lips; your iniquity is taken away, and your sin purged." (Isaiah 6:5-7)

Isaiah's mouth was purified with fire so that the holy Word of God could be spoken by his human lips. In one powerful move, the Lord took away all of the iniquity in His newly commissioned messenger. At the same time, all of his sin was purged so that he could be a clean vessel to receive, carry and speak the Word of the Lord. Isaiah had a clear perspective on his shortcomings and felt totally inadequate to bring the Word of the Lord to a people equally unworthy to receive it. Isaiah couldn't see a solution to the problem, but the Lord knew exactly what to do. He sent an angel with a coal of fire to heal the breach.

The result of this encounter with the fire of God made it possible for Isaiah to let the people know that the Lord wanted to draw close to them and He wanted to cleanse them so they could freely draw close to Him. This message is unchanged. We still need the fire of God to cleanse and purify our hearts and mouths so that we can draw close and be made ready to do His work. The people we minister to also need the fire of God to burn away their iniquity and sin so that they can become carriers of the Spirit of God. If you need God's fire for these same purposes, this is a good time to ask and receive what you need.

FIERY TRIALS WHICH REFINE

In this you greatly rejoice, though now for a little while you may have had to suffer grief in all kinds of trials. These have come so that your faith—of greater worth than gold, which perishes even though refined by fire— may be proved genuine and may result in praise, glory and honor when Jesus Christ is revealed. (1 Peter 1:6-7, NIV)

Many of us have gone through some fiery trials which were very unpleasant at the time. As we look back on them, we can see something like Peter described in the passage above. These trials test our faith as gold is tested in the fire. The product which comes through the fire is now pure and proven. After the fire, we are suddenly able to give pure praise, glory and honor to the Lord. Peter tells us that the end result will be that we can greatly rejoice over being made ready for His service. This is a tough lesson for people and the weak seldom pass the test. Those who finish the course are so much better for having endured and persevered.

BEWARE OF UNAUTHORIZED FIRE

> *Likewise the tongue is a small part of the body, but it makes great boasts. Consider what a great forest is set on fire by a small spark. The tongue also is a fire, a world of evil among the parts of the body. It corrupts the whole person, sets the whole course of his life on fire, and is itself set on fire by hell.* (James 3:5-6, NIV)

In addition to holy fire, there is the possibility of unholy fire. James sees the tongue in our mouths as a source of fire. It can release evil which injures and destroys others or it can release blessings to build people up, strengthen them, and give comfort. The tongue which releases unholy fire is like a two edged sword. It cuts both ways. It not only harms the target of its attacks but also corrupts the *"whole person"* who speaks evil. James says this kind of fire is started by hell itself and can destroy the course of your whole life. Releasing unholy fire can be hazardous to your health.

> *Nadab and Abihu, however, fell dead before the LORD when they made an offering with unauthorized fire before him in the Desert of Sinai. They had no sons; so only Eleazar and Ithamar served as priests during the lifetime of their father Aaron.* (Numbers 3:4)

The things which proceed from our mouths can be a form of "unauthorized fire." We must learn to tame and control the tongue so that the fire will always serve the Lord's purposes and bless His people. How are you doing with your tongue? Does it release more good than evil? Does it bless or curse? We need to examine ourselves and be certain that we are using the fire according to the Lord's will and purposes in our lives and ministries. Consider what the Lord said to Jeremiah. *Therefore thus says the Lord God of hosts: "Because you speak this word, behold, I will make My words in your mouth fire, and this people wood, and it shall devour them."* (Jeremiah 5:14)

The Lord put holy fire in Jeremiah's mouth to deal with those who released unholy fire with their tongues. There is an old adage, "fight fire with fire." This seems to be the mission given to Jeremiah. People today tend to be very casual about what comes out of their mouths. In many churches, I have experienced people judging and accusing other believers and leaders with reckless abandon. I am always apprehensive about this behavior because I remember clearly the prophetic words the Lord gave to Jeremiah. I pray that this type of judgment will not come to you or to me.

> *Then the prophet Jeremiah said to Hananiah the prophet, "Hear now, Hananiah, the LORD has not sent you, but you make this people trust in a lie. Therefore thus says the LORD: 'Behold, I will cast you from the face of the earth. This year you shall die, because you have taught rebellion against the LORD.'"* (Jeremiah 28:15-16)

FIRE AS A TEST OF FAITH

A time of testing has been set for each of us. We need to walk in wisdom at all times and let our actions be tempered in the fear of the Lord. It is an awesome responsibility to be called to speak the Word of the Lord. You must not become casual with your words. You must humbly seek the wisdom and guidance of the Lord to properly carry the fire of His Word to those assigned to you for ministry. You must always stand on the one sure foundation which is Yeshua ha Messiach.

> *And he sent messengers on ahead, who went into a Samaritan village to get things ready for him; but the people there did not welcome him, because he was heading for Jerusalem. When the disciples James and John saw this, they asked, "Lord, do you want us to call fire down from heaven to destroy them?" But Jesus turned and rebuked them, and they went to another village.* (Luke 9:52-56, NIV)

Jesus did not rebuke James and John to punish them. He rebuked them so they would learn not to release unauthorized fire. When you want to release judgment fire because of your hurt feelings or perceived injury, you are in danger of releasing the wrong kind of fire. It is important to wait and follow the word of the Lord. Always remember that fire comes to test those who are standing on and proclaiming the truth of the Word of God. Fire comes to reveal the things of the heart and the quality of your commitment to Him. Fire comes to refine and purify the hearts of the Lord's people. Yeshua released fiery words of rebuke in order to purify His faithful disciples.

Remember what Yeshua said in Luke 12:49 (NIV), "*I have come to bring fire on the earth, and how I wish it were already kindled*! The Day of the Lord is coming when the light of His glory will reveal all things whether good or evil. How will you stand on that day? Consider what the Lord spoke through the prophet Malachi about that day in Malachi 3:2, "*But who can endure the day of His coming? And who can stand when He appears? For He is like a refiner's fire and like launderers' soap.*" I am not asking these questions to cause fear, but to challenge each one to focus on his or her own works and to ensure that they are standing on the one sure foundation.

> *For no one can lay any foundation other than the one already laid, which is Jesus Christ. If any man builds on this foundation using gold, silver, costly stones, wood, hay or straw, his work will be shown for what it is, because the Day will bring it to light. It will be revealed with fire, and the fire will test the quality of each man's work. If what he has built survives, he will receive his reward. If it is burned up, he will suffer loss; he himself will be saved, but only as one escaping through the flames.* (1 Corinthians 3:11-15, NIV)

FIRE AS A SIGN

The Lord uses fire as a sign of His appointed times and seasons. Peter shared a well know prophecy in order to describe what happened on the Day of Pentecost. This prophecy was first given through the prophet Joel. You can read Peter's reference in Acts 2:19 (NIV), "*I will show wonders in the heaven above and signs on the earth below, blood and fire and billows of smoke.*" Those who gathered in Jerusalem that day had experienced a solar eclipse while Yeshua hung on the cross followed by a blood moon on the first night of Passover. These signs were soon followed by the release of great power from the Lord upon the disciples. Luke described what they had experienced in the fourth chapter of the book of Acts. *They saw what seemed to be tongues of fire that separated and came to rest on each of them. All of them were filled with the Holy Spirit and began to speak in other tongues as the Spirit enabled them.* (Acts 2:3-4, NIV)

This was the fulfillment of a great promise given by the Lord centuries before. Yeshua called it the "promise of the Father." This was a direct reference to a promise given in the Passover Seder. In Luke 24:48 we see the release of this promise: "*And you are witnesses of these things. Behold, I send the Promise of My Father upon you; but tarry in the city of Jerusalem until you are endued with power from on high.*" Have you received this promise? Have you received the fire of the Lord which comes with Holy Spirit baptism? If you have not received this glorious infilling, then now is a good time to ask and receive what the Father promised. When it comes, it will be like having your hair set on fire by the tongues of flames. It will be like the fire in the bones described by Jeremiah.

> *Then I said, "I will not make mention of Him, nor speak anymore in His name." But His word was in my heart like a burning fire shut up in my bones; I was weary of holding it back, and I could not.* (Jeremiah 20:9)

TIME TO BE ENDUED WITH FIRE

This is the season for all those who would follow the leadership of the Holy Spirit to be endued with fire and to receive that power from on high. A fire of judgment is coming and we need to go through the fire now so there is nothing left to be burned in that season. Receive the promise of the Lord in Isaiah 43:2, "*When you pass through the waters, I will be with you; and when you pass through the rivers, they will not sweep over you. When you walk through the fire, you will not be burned; the flames will not set you ablaze.*"

Fire is important in the work of the Lord. He calls each of us to go through the fire of purification to be made ready for His service. I don't want to be like those the Lord spoke of in Jeremiah 6:29 (NIV), "*The bellows blow fiercely to burn away the lead with fire, but the refining goes on in vain; the wicked are not purged out.*" It is time for each of us to be purged in the fire of the Lord. I want to be a part of the "third" prophesied by Zechariah. *This third I will bring into the fire; I will refine them like silver and test them like gold. They will call on my name and I will answer them; I will say, "They are my people," and they will say, "The Lord is our God.*" (Zechariah 13:9, NIV) I want each of us to be called "*my people*" by Father God. I want us to be able to truthfully say, "*The Lord is our God.*" Read the passage below aloud over and over until it becomes yours. As you speak it over and over, be in a posture to receive the fire and to be made ready to do His work. Amen?

PRAYER

Grace and peace be multiplied to you in the knowledge of God and of Jesus our Lord, as His divine power has given to us all things that pertain to life and godliness, through the knowledge of Him who called us by glory and virtue, by which have been given to us exceedingly great and precious promises, that through these you may be partakers of the divine nature, having escaped the corruption that is in the world through lust. But also for this very reason, giving all diligence, add to your faith virtue, to virtue knowledge, to knowledge self-control, to self-control perseverance, to perseverance godliness, to godliness brotherly kindness, and to brotherly kindness love. For if these things are yours and abound, you will be neither barren nor unfruitful in the knowledge of our Lord Jesus Christ. For he who lacks these things is shortsighted, even to blindness, and has forgotten that he was cleansed from his old sins. Therefore, brethren, be even more diligent to make your call and election sure, for if you do these things you will never stumble; for so an entrance will be supplied to you abundantly into the everlasting kingdom of our Lord and Savior Jesus Christ. (2 Peter 1:2-11)

AN IMPORTANT REMINDER

Do not quench the Spirit. Do not despise prophecies. (1 Thessalonians 5:19-20)

PAUSE AND REFLECT

1. What do you make of the frequent uses of fire in the scriptures?

2. In what ways does the Lord use fire to accomplish His purposes?

3. What is "the promise of the Father" mentioned by Yeshua?

4. Describe one of your experiences with the fire of the Lord.

5. What is the relationship between fire and the tongue?

6. What are some of the consequences of quenching the fire of the Holy Spirit?

7. What benefits did you receive from the baptism of fire?

CHAPTER TWO

PREPARING HEARTS FOR FIRE

Vision Report
Eagles of Glory

This morning, I was lifted up and positioned under an open heaven watching as the Lord released great fiery glory upon the earth. In the midst of the glory, I saw huge eagles being released to carry the glory to various places. I saw the glory go specifically to South Korea, Israel, and the I-77 corridor of South Carolina. As I watched these powerful eagles moving quickly from heaven to those below who are open, receptive, and willing to be led by the Holy Spirit in the fire of revival, the Word of God began to open in my spirit.

Consider carefully the word of the Lord given in Exodus 19:4, "*You have seen what I did to the Egyptians, and how I bore you on eagles' wings and brought you to Myself.*" The power of God is being released once again to liberate the children of Israel from physical oppression and bondage to a religious spirit. The Lord is carrying them on eagle's wings to the place of His promise for their final restoration. Eagles are also being released to many other nations. This release of His eagles of glory to the nations speaks of this promise being made available for all those who put their trust in the Lord.

> *Even youths grow tired and weary, and young men stumble and fall; but those who hope in the LORD will renew their strength. They will soar on wings like eagles; they will run and not grow weary, they will walk and not be faint.* (Isaiah 40:30-31, NIV)

I heard the voice of the Lord as He called aloud to His people: "Now is the time to rise on wings like eagles. Now is the time to rise above small front line skirmishes. Now is the time to soar above the battle field and see where the real center of battle is currently located." It is time to rise above petty squabbles into the pure air of the Lord's presence and to gain understanding of His strategic plans. It is time for those who serve the Lord to be accelerated toward their real purpose in the kingdom and for them to begin to function out of the wisdom and revelation that comes through the Holy Spirit.

As I continued to watch the eagles, I noticed the effect of their wings on the glory fire of the Lord. The wind beneath their wings was stirring up the glory and causing it to move like a whirlwind. I saw the whirlwind then spread out over all the areas where the eagles were flying. Each one was stirring up the fire of the Lord's glory and kindling flames of revival around the earth. And those who responded to the call by rising on the wings of eagles were each causing additional whirlwinds of the glory of God. As more and more of the faithful rose, the fires spread over their churches, cities, and nations.

At this point, I remembered Luke 12:49, "*I came to send fire on the earth, and how I wish it were already kindled!*"

The spread of this fire has been the Lord's plan for a very long time. We are blessed to live in an age when it is being kindled stronger than ever before. Remember what the Lord spoke through Ezekiel 20:48 (NIV), *"Everyone will see that I the LORD have kindled it; it will not be quenched."* For those who are not submitted to the Lord, it will be the fire of judgment. But, for those who are totally committed to Him, it will be a fire of purification and power. Two powerful passages of scripture came to me. Study both of them and allow the Lord to speak into your heart and release His fire in your life and ministry.

> *Therefore, the Lord, the LORD Almighty, will send a wasting disease upon his sturdy warriors; under his pomp a fire will be kindled like a blazing flame. The Light of Israel will become a fire, their Holy One a flame; in a single day it will burn and consume his thorns and his briers. The Lord gave this prophetic word through Isaiah, "In that day the survivors of the house of Jacob, will no longer rely on him who struck them down but will truly rely on the LORD, the Holy One of Israel."* (Isaiah 10:16-17, NIV)

> *Who may ascend into the hill of the Lord? Or who may stand in His holy place? He who has clean hands and a pure heart, who has not lifted up his soul to an idol, nor sworn deceitfully. He shall receive blessing from the Lord, and righteousness from the God of his salvation. This is Jacob, the generation of those who seek Him, who seek Your face. (Selah) Lift up your heads, O you gates! And*

be lifted up, you everlasting doors! And the King of glory shall come in. Who is this King of glory? The Lord strong and mighty, the Lord mighty in battle. (Psalm 24:3-8)

May the Lord bless you with a powerful release of His glory and cause you to rise on the wings of eagles! May the Lord bless you to be part of the generation of Jacob! May the Lord give you an intense desire to seek Him with all your heart and to see His face! May you see His glory! In the fire of His glory may you see Him as He truly is! May you rise up with those prepared to usher in this great end time harvest! Amen!

(End of Vision Report)

FIRE EXTINQUISHERS VS. FLAME THROWERS

What are you doing with the fire of God? Are you a carrier of the fire? Are you a fire starter? The Lord desires to kindle a fire and He said that we would do what He was doing and even greater things (see John 14:12). Are you starting fires or putting them out? Many people are inadvertently working to extinguish the fires of revival. Most have no idea what they are doing. We have been called to be awake and alert in these last days. If you want to be part of the harvest and to carry the fire of God, begin to ask and seek with all your heart. Remember James' warning and avoid an outcome of not having the things of God in your own life and ministry. *You do not have because you do not ask God. When you ask, you do not receive, because you ask with wrong motives, that you may spend what you get on your pleasures.* (James 4:2b-3, NIV)

It was a warm summer's day in South Carolina as we entered the church and began to give praise and worship to our wonderful Father God. It was one of those days when you feel His Presence and experience His Glory in extraordinary and powerful ways. I was totally focused on this awesome time with the Lord when a strange message appeared on the screen where the words of the song were being projected. The message scrolled across the screen and simply said. Owner of a blue Toyota with License plate #_____, "YOU ARE PARKED TOO CLOSE TO THE FIRE HYDRANT!"

I immediately recognized a prophetic word in this message! My attention quickly shifted from the music to the message. I immediately understood that there was a message in this for all of us. The Lord was bringing something to our attention and it was so important that He interrupted the worship time. He is asking you and me an important question. Are you parked too close to something that is putting out the fire of the Holy Spirit in your heart?

As I pondered this message in my heart, another prophetic word scrolled across the screen. It simply said, "PLEASE MOVE YOUR VEHICLE!" Now here is another powerful word from the Lord. Are you too close to things in your life which tend to extinguish the fire of God? Think about it? Honestly assess your situation for a moment as I did in that church service. If you begin to see that you are positioned with people or in situations which are blocking the Lord's fire, it is time to do something about it. I was hearing the Lord saying, "Please move your heart away from the Fire extinguishers in your life!" Are you hearing this? It may be time to make some important changes in your life and ministry.

Sometimes those things which extinguish the fire are not on the outside. At times there are attitudes or character traits in your own heart which are blocking the fire of God. These things will hinder you from being able to accomplish what the Lord plans for you. These things will block you from reaching your destiny and accomplishing His purpose in your life. The message, "you are parked too close to the fire hydrant!" may be difficult for us to see and receive because the problem is inside us. Think about the condition of your own heart and then answer the question again. Are you parked too close to something which is putting out the fire of the Holy Spirit in your heart?

A lack of faith can work to extinguish the fire of God in your heart. At other times bitterness, resentment and offense act like fire extinguishers in your spirit. If you are unable to forgive someone, it will tend to quench the Spirit and put out the fire of God. I have come to believe that one of the greatest extinguishers of Holy Spirit fire is having expectations which are too low. Are you having difficulty believing that the things promised in the Word of God are for today? Are you finding it difficult to believe that all these things are for you? These attitudes and character traits will severely limit the power of God in you. If you don't deal with them, they may extinguish His fire in your heart.

THINK ABOUT WHAT YOU EXPECT!
THINK ABOUT WHAT YOU BELIEVE!

Then Jesus said to the centurion, "Go your way; and as you have believed, so let it be done for you." And his servant was healed that same hour." (Matthew 8:13)

I have thought about this passage many times as I ministered to others. I often wonder: What would most Christians receive today if they only got what they believed? I am convinced that many believers would receive nothing, because that is the limit of their beliefs. What would you receive if you only got what your faith confirmed? Remember Romans 10:17, "*So then faith comes by hearing, and hearing by the word of God.*" Think seriously about the teaching below from the book of James. Don't merely read it, think it through. Read aloud the passage several times so that it begins to reside in your own heart. In this way you will make it your own and allow it to release Holy Spirit fire in your spirit.

> *But when he asks, he must believe and not doubt, because he who doubts is like a wave of the sea, blown and tossed by the wind. That man should not think he will receive anything from the Lord; he is a double–minded man, unstable in all he does.* (James 1:6-8, NIV)

May people pray for the things they want, but they don't really expect to receive them. Have you heard people pray like this? They often end these prayers by saying something like: Nevertheless not my will, but your will be done. These words tend to cancel out all the faith which might have been released in the prayer. These words expose an attitude of the heart which says that God doesn't really want to bless you with the things you need or want. This is contrary to the Word of God. We have a wonderful, loving Father God. He wants what is best for us. In fact, He wants more for us than we want for ourselves. Let the words of Jesus release more faith to you, and open your heart to receive.

> *So I say to you, ask, and it will be given to you; seek, and you will find; knock, and it will be opened to you. For everyone who asks*

receives, and he who seeks finds, and to him who knocks it will be opened. If a son asks for bread from any father among you, will he give him a stone? Or if he asks for a fish, will he give him a serpent instead of a fish? Or if he asks for an egg, will he offer him a scorpion? If you then, being evil, know how to give good gifts to your children, how much more will your heavenly Father give the Holy Spirit to those who ask Him! (Luke 11:9-13)

Many of us need to seriously attend to the teaching in James 4:8, "*Draw near to God and He will draw near to you. Cleanse your hands, you sinners; and purify your hearts, you double-minded.*" When you approach the Lord with your prayers, you need to have your hands and heart cleansed and purified so that no unbelief or double-mindedness can be found there. This is not as difficult as it sounds. The Lord has already done this for you on the cross and through His resurrection from the dead. You simply need to accept it by faith and let Him accomplish His purposes in your life. This is a good time to pray and ask the Lord to cleanse and purify everything in your heart.

EXPOSING THE MASQUERADE

For many people who consider themselves to be believers, there are unholy things in their hearts which are masquerading as the things of God. I want to make it very clear that there is a huge difference between knowing that the Lord can do something and believing that He will do it for you. Study the words of Yeshua in the passage below. Read them aloud until they become rooted in your heart. Keep doing it until you no longer ask if he will do it for you! Build up your most holy faith.

> *So He asked his father, "How long has this been happening to him?" And he said, "From childhood. And often he has thrown him both into the fire and into the water to destroy him. But if You can do anything, have compassion on us and help us." Jesus said to him, "If you can believe, all things are possible to him who believes." Immediately the father of the child cried out and said with tears, "Lord, I believe; help my unbelief!"* (Mark 9:21-24)

Another problem is revealed when people believe that hope and faith are the same thing. There would be no need for two words if one would do. Many people are only allowing their hearts to hope for things from the Lord. Even worse, many of them don't truly hold out much hope. Meditate on this passage from Hebrews 11:1, "*Now faith is the substance of things hoped for, the evidence of things not seen.*" Hope has no substance. On the other hand, faith is substance. It is tangible. It is real, and it has the power to bring things into being in your life. Consider what Yeshua said about this kind of faith in the passage below.

> *And suddenly, a woman who had a flow of blood for twelve years came from behind and touched the hem of His garment. For she said to herself, "If only I may touch His garment, I shall be made well." But Jesus turned around, and when He saw her He said, "Be of good cheer, daughter; your faith has made*

*you well." And the woman was made well
from that hour.* (Matthew 9:20-22)

This was not an isolated incident. Yeshua said this to others. Look closely at Mark 10:52, "*Then Jesus said to him, 'Go your way; your faith has made you well.' And immediately he received his sight and followed Jesus on the road.*" Jesus spoke out of His own faith before it manifested for the blind man. Jesus knew something very powerful and He released it to the blind man. He has also released it to you and me. Faith is evidence. It is not abstract or vapor. When you receive it by faith in your spirit, you already have it. Faith is knowing that you know, that you know what you have in Christ. When we have Christ-like faith, we begin to realize that faith is possessing things before they manifest in the natural. It is this faith which brings things from being spiritual truth into reality in the physical world. But, do you believe this? That is the key.

BUILD UP YOUR LEVEL OF EXPECTATION

We need to build up our level of expectation! How do you do that? First, you need to take hold of the Word of God. Speak it over and over until it takes a firm hold in your spirit. Claim the fullness of the promise in Romans 10:17, "*So then faith comes by hearing, and hearing by the word of God.*" With this in mind, ask yourself again how you can build up your faith and expectancy. Then claim the promise once again. Faith comes by hearing the Word of God. How do you hear it? Someone has to read it aloud. Let that someone be you. You believe what you say more than you believe what I say. Let the words of faith come from your own mouth.

Another way to build up your faith and expectation is to use the power of confession. The Greek word *"homologio,"* which was translated as confession, actually means to say the same thing. What is the "same thing" you want to confess. Confess what God says. Remember, His word never comes back void. It will always accomplish its purpose. Start making decrees based on God's Word. Start speaking all these good things into being. Start receiving them by faith before they manifest in the natural.

STIR UP YOUR FAITH

It is time for the Lord's people to get seriously involved in stirring up their faith. It is also time to stir up your spiritual gifts. Remember that faith is one of the spiritual gifts mentioned by Paul in First Corinthians Chapter Twelve. When you think about faith as a spiritual gift, you realize that you can actually build it up. Think about what Paul said to his spiritual son Timothy in 2 Timothy 1:6, *"Therefore I remind you to stir up the gift of God which is in you through the laying on of my hands."* This passage is worded a little differently in the NIV. 2 Timothy 1:6 (NIV), *"For this reason I remind you to fan into flame the gift of God, which is in you through the laying on of my hands."*

It is time to stir up your gifts and fan them into flame. In conferences, I often ask people to stand up and begin to wave their hands like a fan over their hearts. I believe that we can activate prophetic words and spiritual promises by taking some action steps. Too often people sit around doing nothing while expecting the Lord to do everything for them. Perhaps the Lord is waiting for you to put some of these things into action in your life and ministry. I believe that it is time for God's people to release some Holy Spirit fire! Take a chance and actually fan your hands over your heart. Let the fire of God increase and burn intensely in your life and ministry.

YOUR GOD GIVEN DESTINY

I want you to consider the following declaration very carefully. **It's time to step into your God-given destiny!** Obviously, I don't know the destiny of everyone who will read this book. It is also clear that I don't know the depth of the Lord's plan and purpose in your life. I do, however, believe that the Lord has more for us than we currently know. I believe that His plan for our lives and ministry is greater than our plans. I believe that the destiny He has spoken into our lives is so great that most of us will have trouble accepting all of it at any given moment. This is why the Lord usually reveals these things to us step by step. I am believing with all my heart that it is time for each of us to take another step or perhaps several steps to move closer to our God-given destinies. So, I will decree it again, hopefully with a stronger impact: **It is now time to step into the fullness of your God-given destiny!** Use the power of confession by making the same decree aloud right now.

It is time for you to move into the fullness of the blessing. I want you to have the same assurance Paul had when he wrote Romans 15:29, "*But I know that when I come to you, I shall come in the **fullness of the blessing** of the gospel of Christ.*" When we meet either on this earth or in Heaven, I expect for you to be "in the fullness of the blessing of the gospel of Christ." Amen? Are you ready to walk in this level of anointing and commissioning? Many people are not. A spirit of fear has been released in the body of Christ, and many people are afraid to step out in the fullness of their anointing and the fullness of the Lord's blessing. Remember what Paul said to his spiritual son in 2 Timothy 1:7, *"For God has not given us a spirit of fear, but of power and of love and of a sound mind."* In the mighty name of Yeshua ha Messiach, we cast out every spirit of fear and decree that you will move in power, love and soundness of mind! Amen?

I believe there are at least five dimensions of this fullness of the blessing which has been revealed in what the Apostle Paul wrote. I pray that the Lord will give you a witness in your spirit to these truths as He did for me. I pray that you will go beyond the revelation I received into the fullness of the understanding of these things. I pray that the Spirit of wisdom and revelation will release these things in your spirit and in your mind. I pray that the promised Spirit of truth will reveal all truth to you right now, in Yeshua's name! Amen and Amen! In the paragraphs below, I want to break this promise down into smaller pieces so that you can receive and digest them fully.

1. Romans 15:32, *"...that I may come to you."* This means that you will be enabled to go to the place of God's anointing. It is critically important to be located in the geographical location of your anointing. This place moves from time to time as the Lord directs you in ministry. Always be ready to move with your anointing.

2. Romans 15:30, *"Now I beg you, brethren, through the Lord Jesus Christ, and through the love of the Spirit, that you strive together with me in prayers to God for me,"* This speaks of an enabling from the Lord which will empower us to strive together in prayer. When we reach this level of anointing we will be moving in the unity of spirit and soul.

3. Romans 15:31, "...*that I may be delivered from those in Judea who do not believe, and that my service for Jerusalem may be acceptable to the saints,*" The fullness of the blessing means that you will be delivered from the power and influence of those who try to hinder your gifts and ministry. Remember that the person set free by the Lord is free indeed!

4. Romans 15:32, "*that I may come to you with joy by the will of God,*" There is no drudgery in the fullness of the blessing. When the Lord blesses you with this anointing, you are enabled to constantly move in joy. This is the will of God. Remember the promise in Nehemiah 8:10, "...*the joy of the LORD is your strength.*"

5. Romans 15:32, "*may be refreshed together with you*" The fullness of the blessing brings you into a season of refreshing. This is not something you enjoy off by yourself somewhere. It is the refreshing which comes when we are in unity with other believers. We are refreshed together.

After releasing this powerful word, Paul finishes with a blessing. I want to release that same blessing to you. Romans 15:33, "*Now the God of peace be with you all. Amen.*" May you always walk in the sevenfold Shalom of God: peace, provision, protection, prosperity, productivity, power, and prophetic words to guide you! This is the fullness of the blessing the Lord desires to release to you right now! This is the fullness of the blessing that He wants you to walk in all the days of your life as you minister the gospel of the Kingdom. Receive it all in Yeshua's mighty name! Amen and Amen!

TIME TO STIR IT UP

To get all these blessings working in your life and ministry, you need to stir them up! Speak aloud again the words of 2 Timothy 1:6, *"I remind you to stir up the gift of God which is in you through the laying on of my hands."* When you speak this aloud over and over, you anchor it in your heart and it becomes empowered by your faith. It is important for you to do it for yourself. You have received spiritual gifts through the laying on of hands. You have received impartation from many spirit-filled leaders. You have receive an anointing from the Lord. All these things belong to you as gifts from the Lord. Now it is up to you to decide what you will do with them. As for me, I am stirring them up and fanning then into a flame in my heart. Are you ready to do the same? Then it is time to claim the promise released to you in the first letter of John. *"But you have an anointing from the Holy One, and you know all things. I have not written to you because you do not know the truth, but because you know it, and that no lie is of the truth."* (1 John 2:20-21)

PUT YOUR WORDS INTO ACTION!

Remember that prophetic words can be activated by taking some serious action steps. I have met many people who want to receive a prophetic word, but don't want to step into it by faith. They plan to sit around waiting for it to happen. You probably know people like that too. Many people are literally sitting on volumes of prophetic words which have never manifested. People have shown me large three-ringed binders with all the prophetic words famous people have spoken over them, but all they are doing is collecting and showing these things to others. If you want these prophecies to manifest, you must step out and begin to act in accordance with the word. This is how you release your faith. Your faith steps will release the power of God to make these things manifest and increase. Now is the time to step into them.

This may sound strange, but I encourage you to stand up wherever you are, and begin to stir up these gifts of God in your own heart! Stir it up! Stir it up! People may look at you with strange facial expressions. That is okay. It will open up an opportunity for you to witness to them about the spiritual gifts the Lord has placed in you. This may release these gifts in them. Remember what is promised in Revelation 19:10, *"For the testimony of Jesus is the spirit of prophecy."* Be strong and courageous as you begin to fan these things into a flame (2 Timothy 1:6, NIV, *"For this reason I remind you to **fan into flame** the gift of God, which is in you through the laying on of my hands."* It is time to get fired up for the Lord and for the gospel of the Kingdom. It is time to release the mighty fire of the Holy Spirit. Begin to fan it into a flame! Fan it, now and keep on fanning it! Let the power of God's fire become a blazing furnace in your own heart. Amen?

I pray for you to receive all this through the laying on of hands. You can actually do this for yourself. We don't need to look for the man or woman of God. We need to be seeking the God of these spirit-filled men and women who are known to have these powerful spiritual gifts. God will bless you through the laying on of your own hands. I know. I have done it many time. Every day, I like to lay hands on myself for the renewing of my mind. When I do this, I feel the fire of God and my head literally burns with His presence and power. I encourage you to do the same. Accept it by faith and then lay hands on yourself to impart more of the fire of God into your own heart.

PRAYER

I beseech you therefore, brethren, by the mercies of God, that you present your bodies a living sacrifice, holy, acceptable to God, which is your reasonable service. ²And do not be conformed to this world, but be transformed by the renewing of your mind, that you may prove what is that good and acceptable and perfect will of God. (Romans 12:1-2) *I have not stopped giving thanks for you, remembering you in my prayers. I keep asking that the God of our Lord Jesus Christ, the glorious Father, may give you the Spirit of wisdom and revelation, so that you may know him better. I pray also that the eyes of your heart may be enlightened in order that you may know the hope to which he has called you, the riches of his glorious inheritance in the saints, and his incomparably great power for us who believe. That power is like the working of his mighty strength, which he exerted in Christ when he raised him from the dead and seated him at his right hand in the heavenly realms, far above all rule and authority, power and dominion, and every title that can be given, not only in the present age but also in the one to come. And God placed all things under his feet and appointed him to be head over everything for the church, which is his body, the fullness of him who fills everything in every way.* (Ephesians 1:16-23, NIV) Amen and Amen!!!

PAUSE AND REFLECT

1. In the next few days, what do you expect to receive from the Lord?

2. Will you step into the fire of the Holy Spirit?

3. How will you begin to carry this fire?

4. In what ways will you become a fire starter for the Lord?

5. How can you help to start the fires of revival, now?

6. How can you stir up the fire of the Holy Spirit which is in you?

CHAPTER THREE

DON'T FEAR THE FIRE

Vision Report
Wall of Fire

During a glory outpouring, we were all intensely caught up in praise and worship. As I was standing among those in the front, I looked to one side of the room and saw an open vision. In other words, I saw it with my eyes wide open. Suddenly, I could not see the people crowded around me. All I could see was a wall of fire which had formed on one side of the worship center. It was about twenty five feet high and about thirty five feet wide. I could feel the heat from the fire and smell the intense burning. Then I heard the Lord say: "Walk through the fire." To say that I was hesitant would be an understatement.

In this open vision, I began to move slowly toward the wall of fire. As I moved closer, I could feel an increase in the temperature in the room. It was very hot and getting hotter with each step. As I got near the wall of fire, it was extremely hot and seemed very real and extremely dangerous. The Lord said again, "Walk through the fire." I was very concerned because it was so real that I sensed that I might die in the fire. I asked the Lord if He was certain that He wanted me to walk through the fire. I was assured that this was the Lord's command.

The heat and smell of the fire was so strong that I was not certain that I would survive a walk through this wall. I thought about Moses' walk up the mountain and into the fire of God's presence. Exodus 20:18-19, "*Now all the people witnessed the thunderings, the lightning flashes, the sound of the trumpet, and the mountain smoking; and when the people saw it, they trembled and stood afar off. Then they said to Moses, "You speak with us, and we will hear; but let not God speak with us, lest we die."* The people were too afraid to step out in faith. Because of their fear and reluctance, they missed the awesome things the Lord had prepared for them. I did not want to make the same mistake.

I was very close to the wall at this point. I thought: If I die, I die and I will be with the Lord. I took a deep breath and moved toward the fire. It only took one step to be in the midst of the intense flames which seemed to be leaping upward toward the ceiling of the worship center. I took another step and moved completely through the fire. I did not feel any of my flesh burning, but I knew that something had changed. Some things which had been in my spirit and soul before the fire were gone. I was no longer afraid of the fire, but was filled with joy because of what the Lord had done for me.

I shared this experience in the meeting which followed the praise and worship. I was filled with a desire to encourage people to let go of all their fear of the fire of the Lord. I wanted everyone to have this wonderful experience of allowing the Lord to burn away everything which hinders their walk with Him. I still have a strong desire to release this message to others. I feel joy as I write this to you, the reader. I pray that you too will encounter the Lord as a consuming fire which refines and purifies you. I pray that as you go through the fire you will be better equipped to serve in the Kingdom of God. Amen and Amen!

(End of Vision Report)
FEAR OF FIRE

Again, he sent a third captain of fifty with his fifty men. And the third captain of fifty went up, and came and fell on his knees before Elijah, and pleaded with him, and said to him: "Man of God, please let my life and the life of these fifty servants of yours be precious in your sight. Look, fire has come down from heaven and burned up the first two captains of fifties with their fifties. But let my life now be precious in your sight." (2 Kings 1:13-14)

Fire is a frightening thing for most people. The third captain of fifty men was obviously afraid of the fire of God which Elijah had called down on the previous two captains. In Elijah's day most of the people in Israel had lost their fear of God and their fear of His fire. The leaders in Israel had all become very arrogant and rebellious against the Lord. In Judah there had been a mixture of good and bad kings, but in Israel they were all bad. Most of them hated the prophets because they didn't want to hear the truth. Through the ministry of Elijah, the Lord had rekindled their fear of His fire and His judgment. They had seen the fire of God come down on Mount Carmel and burn up the sacrifice, the stone altar, and the water on and around the sacrifice. Now they had seen the fiery judgment of God falling on two proud and rebellious captains and the warriors they led. The Lord humbled the third one so that Elijah could safely travel with Him.

From a very early age most people are taught and learn to fear fire. Young children quickly understand the foolishness of disobeying their parent's commands not to touch hot things. The truth is that fire can bring intense pain. These lessons about fire and the consequences of touching it come on multiple levels of learning. The first level of this learning is that fire brings pain. The next level is to learn that fire destroys. There is also a pain that comes from loss. Fire can destroy precious things which may not be replaceable. I learned as a chaplain on the burn ward of a major hospital that skin and even limbs can be lost as a result of fire. Disfigurement comes and brings a loss of one's appearance and to some degree their personal identity. It is necessary and good for us to teach our children to avoid fire.

One of the tough lessons for many children is to avoid playing with matches. As a young child visiting a friend, I learned this the hard way. My friend had taken a box of matches from the kitchen and led me outside into a field of very dry sage grass. Hidden by the tall grass, we could break the rules and demonstrate that we were completely capable of using matches for fun and with no bad outcomes. This turned out to be a very dangerous mistake. In a short period of time, our fire was out of control. We were barely able to escape without injury. Others had to rush to put out the fire before it spread to the property of others. You may also have very stark and painful memories of the lessons you have learned about avoiding the harmful effects of fire. This fear is good when it provides a layer of protection over us.

Unfortunately, this fear often impedes the progress of believers in properly handling the fire of God. If you are in a right relationship with the Lord, you have nothing to fear from His fire. If you are being led by the Holy Spirit, you have everything to gain from the fire of God. In these fiery experiences we can encounter the Lord coming to us in glory and great power. Fearing God's fire can prevent you from seeing and understanding some of the most intense and exciting experiences possible with the Lord. Think about what the Hebrews missed in the wilderness when the Lord invited them to draw close to Him. Their fear blocked them from experiencing many of the awesome things the Lord was doing in their midst.

> *Then it came to pass on the third day, in the morning, that there were thunderings and lightnings, and a thick cloud on the mountain; and the sound of the trumpet was very loud, so that all the people who were in the camp trembled. And Moses brought the people out of the camp to meet with God, and they stood at the foot of the mountain.* (Exodus 19:16-17)

When we feel in danger, most of us want the fire and power of God to come and rescue us. We would like to be able to fight the fiery attacks of our enemies with the consuming fire of God. There are times when we would like to have a cloud by day and a column of fire by night to lead us and protect us. The children of Israel loved these manifestations of the Lord's presence and power, but they wanted to see it from a distance. When it came to drawing close to the Lord, whom they described as a "consuming fire," they wanted to stand at a safe distance. Each of us needs to evaluate our own responses to the

Lord and see if our fear is preventing us from experiencing the awesome presence and power of the Lord.

Sometimes, believers are frightened when they get a glimpse of the Lord's power. Most believers have only seen or experienced a small portion of His fire and His power. Yet, it is enough to frighten them away from His presence. I like to look at some of the encounters in the Old Testament and try to envision them happening to me. I want to honestly look at my own responses to the Lord and compare them to the actions taken by those in the Biblical accounts. I encourage you to go back to these passages of scripture and try to visualize yourself in their place. Would you have responded differently? Most people quickly and bravely decree that they would have responded in a different way. When I hear this I think about the bravado of Peter before he met the enemy in the garden. "*Peter answered and said to Him, 'Even if all are made to stumble because of You, I will never be made to stumble.' Jesus said to him, 'Assuredly, I say to you that this night, before the rooster crows, you will deny Me three times.'*" (Matthew 26:33-34)

What we learn from Peter's experience is that we are all capable of letting fear block us from fulfilling our promises to the Lord. We were created with a strong drive for safety and survival. It takes great faith to overcome this natural and God-given fear response. This is why we need to read the Word of God and His promises of protection over and over. This is why we need to read them aloud often. This is why Paul taught in Romans 10:17, "*So then faith comes by hearing, and hearing by the word of God.*" You need to practice your sword drills before the battle begins. After the battle starts it is too late to practice and improve your faith skills. Remember "*...take the helmet of salvation, and the sword of the Spirit, which is the word* *of God.* The Word of God is our sword of the Spirit. Now that you are armed and trained for battle, look again at the description of how the Lord appeared on Mount Sinai.

> *Now Mount Sinai was completely in smoke, because the Lord descended upon it in fire. Its smoke ascended like the smoke of a furnace, and the whole mountain quaked greatly.* (Exodus 19:18)

In the earthquake, the fire and the smoke how strong is your faith? Will you stand in faith or in fear? Will you stand with a combination of both? I think that when we are honest about our spiritual condition, most will admit that they carry a combination of faith and fear. We don't have to stay in that condition which predisposes us to fail the test of faith. We need to stand on the Word of God and cast out all fear. Speak over and over the words of 2 Timothy 1:7, *"For God has not given us a spirit of fear, but of power and of love and of a sound mind."* It is important to always remember that fear comes from bondage to sin with the accompanying fear of judgment and condemnation. Now is the time to grasp and hold on to the powerful and liberating Word of God. Remember: *"There is therefore now no condemnation to those who are in Christ Jesus, who do not walk according to the flesh, but according to the Spirit. For the law of the Spirit of life in Christ Jesus has made me free from the law of sin and death."* (Romans 8:1-2)

FEAR CAN CAUSE YOU TO MISS WHAT GOD HAS FOR YOU

Fear not, for I am with you; be not dismayed, for I am your God. I will strengthen you, yes, I will help you, I will uphold you with My righteous right hand. (Isaiah 41:10)

The Lord's presence (with fire and power) is intended to produce faith rather than fear. "*There is no room in love for fear. Well-formed love banishes fear. Since fear is crippling, a fearful life—fear of death, fear of judgment—is one not yet fully formed in love.*" (1 John 4:18, TMSG) Debilitating fear is a sign of immaturity in the faith. It demonstrates that we have not yet been perfected in the love of God. When the perfect love of God the Father fills our hearts, there is no room left for fear. It pushes all of it out.

FEAR CAN CAUSE YOU TO MISS YOUR CALLING

Moses experienced an appropriate kind of fear when he came into the presence of a holy God. His fear was more like the English word "awe." He was in awe of who God is, what He has done, what He is doing, and what He promises to do in the future. You quickly see the difference between Moses' fear and the fear experienced by the children of Israel. Moses didn't let fear or the fire keep him from his destiny. When the Lord called, Moses drew near.

Real spiritual warriors run toward the sound of battle rather than away from it. They experience fear, but they overcome it with the courage which comes from knowing that the Lord is with them. Moses didn't run or hide from the fire of God. Moses walked toward the fire to discover what God had for him. What will you do when you are faced with the fire of God? Moses heard the Lord calling and he answered the call.

> *And when the blast of the trumpet sounded long and became louder and louder, Moses spoke, and God answered him by voice. Then the Lord came down upon Mount Sinai, on the top of the mountain. And the Lord called Moses to the top of the mountain, and Moses went up.* (Exodus 19:19-20)

FEAR CAN CAUSE YOU TO MISS YOUR MOMENT WITH GOD

Imagine how different the outcome would have been if Moses had not gone up into the fire and the presence of the Lord. The story of his life would not have been included in the Word of God. He would not be known as the great prophet who foreshadowed the coming of Yeshua ha Messiach as the redeemer. Perhaps the Lord would have found another way to draw Moses into the fire. It is more likely that the Lord would have found someone else to do His bidding. Moses could have missed out on that forty plus years of walking in intimacy and fellowship with the Lord. He may never have experienced the Lord speaking to him face to face as a man with his friend. The lives of so many others in that time demonstrate the great loss when you fail to answer the Lord's call and commissioning. Look again at how most of them responded.

> *Now all the people witnessed the thunderings, the lightning flashes, the sound of the trumpet, and the mountain smoking; and when the*

people saw it, they trembled and stood afar off. Then they said to Moses, "You speak with us, and we will hear; but let not God speak with us, lest we die." (Exodus 20:18-19)

God invited them up on the mountain for an awesome encounter, but fear kept them back. They thought they had a better idea. They would send Moses and wait to see if he survived in the atmosphere of so much of God's Glory. They made a foolish mistake and spoke a vow they could not or would not perform. They agreed to do whatever the Lord told Moses. As you know, they didn't keep that vow. Rebellion was more powerful in their hearts than their desire to be obedient.

I have often wondered what would have happened if they had responded differently. What if they had gone up into the Lord's presence? What if they experienced more of what Moses received? Would their lives have been different? Would they have been able to enter the Promised Land? We will never know, because they failed the test over and over. Fear caused them to reject the Lord's amazing and wonderful invitation. As they came near the entrance to the Promised Land, Moses reminded them of what they had done.

So it was, when you heard the voice from the midst of the darkness, while the mountain was burning with fire, that you came near to me, all the heads of your tribes and your elders. And you said: "Surely the Lord our God has shown us His glory and His greatness, and we have heard His voice from the midst of the fire. We have seen this day that God speaks with man; yet he still lives. Now therefore, why should we die? For this great fire will consume us; if we hear the voice of the Lord our God anymore, then we shall die." (Deuteronomy 5:23-25)

Instead of faithfully obeying the Lord's instructions, they sent Moses to stand in for them. Think about all they missed. They could have soaked in His glory. They might have experienced a deeper level of His love and grace. They might have learned personally from His great self-disclosure of His nature and character. They would have remained in the flow of God's release of their destiny. They would today be known for what they saw and experienced in the glory. They would have paved the way for an entire generation of those who seek His face.

Who may ascend into the hill of the Lord? Or who may stand in His holy place? He who has clean hands and a pure heart, who has not lifted up his soul to an idol, nor sworn deceitfully. He shall receive blessing from the Lord, and righteousness from the God of his salvation. This is Jacob, the generation of those who seek Him, who seek Your face. Selah (Psalm 24:3-6)

Looking closely at the words in Psalm 24 gives you a clear picture of a different outcome which would have been available for the children of Israel. The words, *"This is Jacob"* is a direct reference to Israel since both names are related to the same man. Jacob courageously wrestled with the Lord and emerged with the name Israel. Many people are still merely trying to return to the level of Jacob. It is good that they are seeking the Lord, however the promise of the Lord is much higher. The spiritual goal is to become like Israel. It points to those who have met God and have overcome their weaknesses and fear.

The failure of the children of Israel also points out another one of the problems they needed to deal with before meeting with the Lord. Their hands were not clean and their hearts were not pure at that time. You are so blessed because you know Yeshua ha Messiach. As you put your faith in Him, your hands are cleansed and your heart is purified by what He did on the cross for you. Because of Yeshua ha Messiach you can ascend the "hill of the Lord." Because of what Yeshua did, you can be a part of the "generation of those who seek" and find the Lord. Amen?

> *For who is there of all flesh who has heard the voice of the living God speaking from the midst of the fire, as we have, and lived? You go near and hear all that the Lord our God may say, and tell us all that the Lord our God says to you, and we will hear and do it.* (Deuteronomy 5:26-27)

Fear robbed them of their moment with the Lord. Fear caused them to stay behind and miss the glory. Fear caused them to remain at a distance for the rest of their lives. Fear is powerful and it can rob you of your destiny in the Lord. Don't allow this to happen to you. God's plan is for you to overcome fear because of His presence. God's plan is to give you His "perfect love" which will cast out all fear. The Lord's destiny for you is to release His fire and power to accompany your ministry for the Kingdom of God.

FEAR CAN CAUSE YOU TO
FAIL A TEST OF FAITH.

And Moses said to the people, "Do not fear; for God has come to test you, and that His fear may be before you, so that you may not sin." So the people stood afar off, but Moses drew near the thick darkness where God was. (Exodus 20:20-21)

Too many people are standing "afar off" today. Rather than accepting what Yeshua did for them on the cross, they are clinging to the fear released by the enemy. I encourage you to read aloud the great teaching on faith found in the Eleventh Chapter of the Book of Hebrews. Let the testimonies of God's faith-filled people of the past release power in your spirit to overcome fear and allow you to accomplish your destiny for the Kingdom.

We should go beyond where they went, because we have something they did not have. We have what Yeshua did for us on the cross. "*God having provided something better for us, that they should not be made perfect apart from us.*" (Hebrews 11:40) Study the passage below and see what you can receive when you let faith overcome your fears. Read the passage aloud over and over until it becomes yours. Take note of the power promised for the Lord's faithful followers.

And what more shall I say? For the time would fail me to tell of Gideon and Barak and Samson and Jephthah, also of David and Samuel and the prophets: who through faith subdued kingdoms, worked righteousness, obtained promises, stopped the mouths of lions, quenched the violence of fire, escaped the edge of the sword, out of weakness were made strong, became valiant in battle, turned to flight the armies of the aliens. Women received their dead raised to life again. (Hebrews 11:32-35a)

As you consider these things, ask yourself some questions. They overcame every attack by the enemy through their faith. How about you? Is your faith giving you deliverance from these things? Notice the powerful words in Hebrews 11:35a. In that day, by the power of faith, people were routinely receiving their dead raised back to life. Would you like to live in a time like that? You can! Now is the time to resurrect that kind of powerful faith. Build up your faith and be ready with a faith-filled answer as I ask again: Are you moving closer to God or standing afar off?

FREEDOM FROM EVERY SPIRIT OF FEAR

All believers need to be set free from every spirit of fear. This is a big generalization and most of us were taught to avoid generalizations. In this case, I believe it is appropriate to break this grammatical rule. Think about it! Some generalizations are true and we can state them boldly and claim them by faith. You can take these promises to the bank. Perfect love casts out all fear. Do you believe this? Consider what the Lord spoke to Israel through the prophet Isaiah.

But now, thus says the Lord, who created you, O Jacob, and He who formed you, O Israel: "Fear not, for I have redeemed you; I

have called you by your name; you are Mine.
When you pass through the waters, I will be
with you; and through the rivers, they shall
not overflow you. When you walk through the
fire, you shall not be burned, nor shall the
flame scorch you. (Isaiah 43:1-2)

If you have a spirit of fear, I want to assure you that it doesn't come from God. Read aloud again what Paul declared to Timothy in 2 Timothy 1:7, *"For God has not given us a spirit of fear, but of power and of love and of a sound mind."* Now think about this. If fear doesn't come from God, where does it come from? I am certain that you know the answer to this question. Fear is a spiritual gift from the enemy. I don't want anything the enemy has to offer. How about you? Everything the enemy gives comes with a heavy price tag. The Lord gives something very different from what the enemy is releasing, and it is all free to those willing to receive it and live by it.

Love has been perfected among us in this:
that we may have boldness in the day of
judgment; because as He is, so are we in this
world. There is no fear in love; but perfect
love casts out fear, because fear involves tor-
ment. But he who fears has not been made
perfect in love. We love Him because He first
loved us. (1 John 4:17-19)

God gives perfect love to those willing to receive it. Let the love of God drive out all of your fears. Don't wait another day. Today is the day of your liberation. Today is the day of the Lord's favor. Today is the day of the Lord's salvation. Today is your independence day. No more fear. No more spirit of fear. Cast it all out by the power of His love. Cast it out in the mighty name of Yeshua ha Messiach. There is great power in that name. Declare it in faith and release the promised power.

> *Therefore God also has highly exalted Him and given Him the name which is above every name, that at the name of Jesus every knee should bow, of those in heaven, and of those on earth, and of those under the earth, and that every tongue should confess that Jesus Christ is Lord, to the glory of God the Father.* (Philippians 2:9-11)

TIME TO DRAW NEAR

> *Draw near to God and He will draw near to you. Cleanse your hands, you sinners; and purify your hearts, you double-minded.* (James 4:8)

Right now, Adonai, the Lord of love, is inviting you to draw near to Him! Are you ready for it? Are you ready to draw near to the Lord? Are you ready to step into the fire of the Holy Spirit? Remember the Lord does not bless cowardly behavior. He has made that very clear. Notice in the passage below that the cowardly go into the lake of fire before murderers, idolaters, liars, and the sexually immoral. "*But the cowardly, unbelieving, abominable, murderers, sexually immoral, sorcerers, idolaters, and all liars shall have their part in the lake which burns with fire and brimstone, which is the second death.*" (Revelation 21:8)

This is the season to seek the Lord's face and become part of the generation of Jacob. This is the season to wait upon the Lord. Think about the promise in Isaiah 40:31, *"But those who wait on the Lord shall renew their strength; they shall mount up with wings like eagles, they shall run and not be weary, they shall walk and not faint."* Don't grow weary being obedient to the Word of the Lord. This is a time to be strengthened in the Lord. The waiting period is the proper time to be set free from fear, empowered by faith, and anointed with a fresh outpouring of the Lord's fire. People tend to give up quickly these days. Think about it. Moses waited forty years to receive an anointing and commissioning by the Lord.

> *And when forty years had passed, an Angel of the Lord appeared to him in a flame of fire in a bush, in the wilderness of Mount Sinai. When Moses saw it, he marveled at the sight; and as he drew near to observe, the voice of the Lord came to him, saying, "I am the God of your fathers—the God of Abraham, the God of Isaac, and the God of Jacob." And Moses trembled and dared not look. Then the Lord said to him, "Take your sandals off your feet, for the place where you stand is holy ground. I have surely seen the oppression of My people who are in Egypt; I have heard their groaning and have come down to deliver them. And now come, I will send you to Egypt."* (Acts 7:30-34)

The fire of punishment is not reserved for those who obediently follow the Lord. The lake of fire is reserved for the devil, the beast, the false prophet and those who choose to follow them. You do not need to fear the fire of the Lord. His fire will cleanse you, purify you, strengthen you and empower you to do His work. Do not be afraid of the fire of God. Embrace it and receive all the Lord has reserved for His faithful followers. You can then stand aside and watch what He has reserved for those who choose to rebel and live in wickedness.

> *Now when the thousand years have expired, Satan will be released from his prison and will go out to deceive the nations which are in the four corners of the earth, Gog and Magog, to gather them together to battle, whose number is as the sand of the sea. They went up on the breadth of the earth and surrounded the camp of the saints and the beloved city. And fire came down from God out of heaven and devoured them. The devil, who deceived them, was cast into the lake of fire and brimstone where the beast and the false prophet are. And they will be tormented day and night forever and ever.* (Revelation 20:7-10)

PRAYER

> *Rejoice in the Lord always. Again I will say, rejoice! Let your gentleness be known to all men. The Lord is at hand. Be anxious for nothing, but in everything by prayer and supplication, with thanksgiving, let your requests be made known to God; and the peace of God, which surpasses all understanding, will guard your hearts and minds through Christ Jesus. Finally, brethren, whatever things are true, whatever things are noble, whatever things are just, whatever things are*

pure, whatever things are lovely, whatever things are of good report, if there is any virtue and if there is anything praiseworthy—meditate on these things. The things which you learned and received and heard and saw in me, these do, and the God of peace will be with you. (Philippians 4:4-9)

PAUSE AND REFLECT

1. If fear does not come from the Lord, where does it come from?

2. Can you remember and describe a time when you were afraid of fire?

3. What can the fire of God do for you?

4. What force of God can set you free from fear? How does it work?

5. How are you made ready to ascend the hill of the Lord?

6. Is your faith giving you deliverance from the spirit of fear?

7. Who are the first to go into the lake of fire? (Revelation 21:6)

CHAPTER FOUR

FIRE WHICH BRINGS POWER!

VISION REPORT
A COLUMN OF FIRE

As I entered the sanctuary during the second session of a Glory Outpouring, I knew immediately that something had shifted in the atmosphere of the worship center. The first session had been very uneventful. I had tried to make things happen on my own rather than just trusting the Lord to move in our midst. Between the sessions I had meditated on what was missing and came under conviction that I was the hindrance to a move of the Lord. I went through a time of intense repentance between the sessions. I cried out to the Lord and committed to standing aside to let Him work. I was hoping and praying that this would not be a repeat of our first meeting.

As I moved through the chairs on the way to my seat at the front, I encountered the power and presence of the Lord. Humility and repentance had opened a door in the spirit realm and I knew the Lord was answering my desperate prayers and was powerfully coming through for us. As I got near the front of the chairs, I felt like I was walking into a wall of power and energy. I couldn't press through it and to be truthful I didn't want to move out of the Presence of the Lord. I stood there a long time and soaked in the Presence as the worship team continued to lead the people. Then I began to move to different sections in the seating area and sensed where the power was manifesting in the strongest ways. It was awesome and wonderful.

The pastor wanted me to move up on the chancel area and to be seated in the chairs reserved for speakers, but I didn't want to go. I wanted to stay on the level where the people were seated and to feel more of His power and presence. What I was receiving from the Lord was so much better than any words I could speak. I didn't want to interrupt the Lord from what He was doing in the midst of those who were praising Him wholeheartedly. I told the pastor that I wanted to wait in that spot, and he acquiesced to my request.

As I stood in awe of the Presence, I looked up at the pulpit. It was high up on the stage and seemed too far from the people and the Presence. As I continued to look at the pulpit, I felt a great resistance in my spirit to taking my place in that part of the sanctuary. Suddenly, an open vision came to me. I saw Heaven open over the pulpit and a column of fire descended rapidly and rested just behind it in the spot where a speaker would stand. Now, I knew that I didn't want to get into that position. The Lord was doing something with fire and it was not a place for any person to stand. I told the pastor what I was seeing and He got very excited about this manifestation. He checked with his seers and they were seeing it too.

The column of fire did not lift for several minutes. Then something began to flow from the bottom of the column of fire. As it moved away from the fire, it turned blue and appeared to be water. I immediately understood in my spirit that the Lord was pouring out living water to revive, refresh and renew His people. When the flow of water came down to where I was standing I could feel the cool refreshing flow up to my ankles. Gradually, it became deeper and was up to the middle of my calves as it moved on up to about knee deep. I shared this with the pastor and he called for his people to come up and stand in the water. Many began to feel the cool refreshing flow of living water. I looked up again at the column of fire and the words of Exodus 3:2-5 came to my mind.

> *And the Angel of the Lord appeared to him in a flame of fire from the midst of a bush. So he looked, and behold, the bush was burning with fire, but the bush was not consumed. Then Moses said, "I will now turn aside and see this great sight, why the bush does not burn." So when the Lord saw that he turned aside to look, God called to him from the midst of the bush and said, "Moses, Moses!" And he said, "Here I am." Then He said, "Do not draw near this place. Take your sandals off your feet, for the place where you stand is holy ground."*

I immediately took off my shoes as I continued to worship. At this point I told the pastor that I would not return to stand behind that pulpit. I asked for a music stand to be placed on the floor level of the sanctuary for me to use as I spoke during this session. I have visited this church many times since this occurred and I have not returned to stand behind that pulpit. For me it is holy ground and I don't want to stand there. The pastor actually purchased a set of two smaller lecterns with wheels and kept them at floor level where I could use them on my visits to the church. There was one for me and one for the translator.

I believe we are being called back to a time for living in awe of the Lord. We are being called to understand the difference between what is holy and what is not. Respect and awe for the Lord draws Him close and I want that most of all. My heart's desire is for you to experience His holy presence and to be totally changed by the fire of His Glory. Are you ready to draw near to Him? Are you ready to move closer even when He manifests as a consuming fire? Amen and Amen!

(End of Vision Report)
THE FOUR ELEMENTS

For everyone will be salted with fire. Salt is good, but if the salt would become salt-less, with what will you season? You have salt in yourselves, and you must continually live in peace with one another. (Mark 9:49-50, ONMB)

The ancient Greek theory of science held that there were four basic elements making up all matter. These four elements were identified as earth, wind, water, and fire. As with many early scientific theories, you may call this one into question. One thing is certain: at least three of these four elements are very powerful forces on the earth. When these forces are released, human beings seem virtually helpless to face them.

I survived an F4 tornado in Oklahoma which hit less than one block from where I stood. At that time I lived near the city of Moore, Oklahoma where many powerful tornadoes have reeked massive damage to lives and manmade structures. If you have experienced this or any other huge storm, you know the power of wind. I witnessed fires burning many things in my hometown as I grew up. An arsonist was in our midst and he was not discovered for many months. We all knew by personal experience the destructive power of fire. Several of my classmates died as a result of drowning in a river near our home. We knew the power of water which often flooded our area as the river overflowed its banks. Perhaps experiences like this were behind the Greek theory of the four elements.

POWERFUL FORCES ON EARTH

Three of the most powerful natural forces on the earth are wind, water and fire. Take a moment and consider all the power released through these basic elements. Wind can be extremely productive or very destructive. Ships have sailed for generations by the power of wind. Much of the world's electrical energy is now produced by wind blowing on gigantic turbines. On the other hand much damage is unleased by the winds in hurricanes, tornadoes, cyclones, and typhoons as well as from straight line winds. Every year billions of dollars in damages occur from these storms and many lives are lost to natures furry released in wind storms.

The power of flowing water is another great source of natural energy which may produce either productive or destructive results. Water is critical to the survival of all life on planet earth. Flowing water moves this essential element from a source to a place of need. A great deal of our electrical energy is produced by hydro-electric power plants harnessing the power of flowing water to turn mighty turbines. On the other hand so much damage is incurred each year from floods, torrential downpours and raging rivers. Have you ever tried to stand up in the ocean turf and resist the flow of powerful waves crashing against your unprotected body? We have so little natural power to withstand the flow of water. At best we have learned to harness it on a limited basis for our own good. On the other hand we have never been able to develop an effective plan to prevent or control flooding, tsunamis or oceanic storms.

Fire is another powerful natural force which is so necessary for our survival and yet capable of being extremely destructive. It takes an extremely hot fire to refine iron ore into steel. The same is true for many other metallic products which are necessary to sustain our modern lifestyles. We need fire to purify, cleanse and shape materials we use in our everyday lives. Fire is essential for cooking our food and preserving substances for later use. On the other hand, most of us have seen or personally experienced the devastating effects of raging fires. Who can forget the pictures of recent wildfires shooting flames several hundred feet in the air as they destroyed everything in their path? Fires account for hundreds if not thousands of home losses each year. Crops are also destroyed by wild fires which can quickly get out of control. The lives of people, livestock and pets are lost more often than we care to remember.

These elements are indeed powerful natural resources. They are descriptive of powerful spiritual forces as well. The Bible uses all three of these elements in describing the work of the Holy Spirit. God wants you to know and feel that power! He wants to wield that power on your behalf and to protect you from the harmful side of these forces. People often have difficulty understanding spiritual forces. The Lord uses these known visible elements to describe unseen and often unknown spiritual forces. You can probably name many of these Biblical references.

Jesus used wind as an example of the movement of the Holy Spirit. Even the well-educated Jewish leader, Nicodemus, had difficulty understanding the things of the spiritual realm. Jesus used the illustration of the wind to help him understand the movements of the Spirit. The Holy Spirit is very mysterious for those who have not yet been baptized in the Spirit and the fire. Study the passage below to see how Jesus used this imagery to help Nicodemus understand.

> *The wind blows wherever it pleases. You hear its sound, but you cannot tell where it comes from or where it is going. So it is with everyone born of the Spirit.* (John 3:8)

Jesus was basically saying, "Like the wind, you don't really know where the Holy Spirit comes from and you don't know where He is going." Some of your natural senses may pick up signals that He is present and His power is being released. You may not understand it, but you know He is at work. You eventually learn that when the Holy Spirit is here and working, you cannot effectively ignore Him. He is more powerful than the wind because He can control the wind. He can do more to help you than the wind can do for you. Likewise, He can destroy the works of evil that you or others may release to those around you.

Jesus often used water to describe the movement and working of the Holy Spirit. The Holy Spirit brings more than just natural water. The Holy Spirit brings living water to flow into us and enliven us. Then the Spirit allows that living water to flow out from us in ministry to others. We don't always fully understand Him, but we know He is here. We also know when He is at work in our lives and ministries.

In fact John tells us in the book of Revelation 5:6 that the seven Spirits of God have been sent into all the earth. "*And I looked, and behold, in the midst of the throne and of the four living creatures, and in the midst of the elders, stood a Lamb as though it had been slain, having seven horns and seven eyes, which are the seven Spirits of God sent out into all the earth.*" If they have been sent into all the earth, they are present with you right now. You can experience the flow of living water brought by the Spirit right now. Read the passage below and claim it for yourself.

> *On the last day, that great day of the feast, Jesus stood and cried out, saying, "If anyone thirsts, let him come to Me and drink. He who believes in Me, as the Scripture has said, out of his heart will flow rivers of living water." But this He spoke concerning the Spirit, whom those believing in Him would receive; for the Holy Spirit was not yet given, because Jesus was not yet glorified."* (John 7:37-39)

If you know and understand the power of a flowing river, you can know and understand many of the workings of the Holy Spirit. The Holy Spirit flows like water into your heart. Then the Holy Spirit will flow from your heart like a powerful river. While the water is flowing through you, let it wash away everything that hinders. Let it wash you clean so that with clean hands and a pure heart you can ascend the hill of the Lord. Let the Holy Spirit cleanse you so that you can walk in greater intimacy with the Lord.

The Lord has also used the element of fire to describe the working and outcomes of the Holy Spirit. As we discussed above, fire is an awesome force which can cleanse and purify or it can destroy. The psalmist saw the Spirit of the Lord working in His prophets to accomplish some similar things. Psalm 104:4 (NIV), "*He makes winds his messengers, flames of fire his servants.*" We need to understand that at times the fires we experience are in fact serving the purposes of the Lord. At other times, they may be His messengers released to help and guide us.

The baptism of fire is intended to accompany the baptism of the Holy Spirit. Many people have experienced water baptism without ever receiving either of the two spiritual baptisms. Remember that fire can refine and purify the hearts and minds of the Lord's people. Isaiah experienced the cleansing of his lips and heart when an angel touched him with a burning coal from the fire of God.

> *So I said: "Woe is me, for I am undone! Because I am a man of unclean lips, and I dwell in the midst of a people of unclean lips; for my eyes have seen the King, The Lord of hosts." Then one of the seraphim flew to me, having in his hand a live coal which he had taken with the tongs from the altar. And he touched my mouth with it, and said: "Behold, this has touched your lips; your iniquity is taken away, and your sin purged."* (Isaiah 6:5-7)

The Lord also made an illustration out of the ability of fire to destroy. The judgment of God has been described as something like the burning of chaff with unquenchable fire. Human might and human power are not adequate to accomplish the purposes of God. To us, His power and the way it manifests may seem overwhelming. We need to understand that the power of the Holy Spirit is far greater than any natural element. Consider this as you study the passage below. This is another good scripture to read aloud until it becomes you own. It is important to remember the real power of God is normally made available to us through the Holy Spirit. "*So he said to me, 'This is the word of the Lord to Zerubbabel: 'Not by might nor by power, but by my Spirit,' says the Lord Almighty.*" (Zechariah 4:6, NIV)

WAIT FOR POWER

When Jesus sent the disciples to Jerusalem to receive the baptism of the Holy Spirit and fire, He told them to wait for power. I have heard many sermons about why the Lord told them to wait. Most of these messages focused on what they did while they waited. The point has been made that these activities were necessary to release this movement of the Spirit. This could not be further from the truth. He was telling them to wait for the Lord's timing. Centuries ago the Lord established Shavuot (Day of Pentecost) as an appointed time for the release of the Holy Spirit and fire. They were to wait for the Lord's timing. In other words, they were waiting for the day when the Father's promise would be released.

> *On one occasion, while he was eating with them, he gave them this command: "Do not leave Jerusalem, but wait for the gift my Father promised, which you have heard me speak about. For John baptized with water, but in a few days you will be baptized with the Holy Spirit.*" (Acts 1:4-5, NIV)

Don't get caught up in all the manmade teachings about the waiting. It doesn't come through our works regardless of how good they may be. It wasn't the waiting that produced the fire. It wasn't anything they did or anything which anyone else can do which will kindle the fire of God. It was what Yeshua did on the cross that initiated this move of God. It was all done by Him in accordance with the Word of God and the promises He released long ago through His prophets. It came as a result of a promise from the Father. It came in His timing. He had the children of Israel preparing and rehearsing for this outpouring all those years on His appointed time of Pentecost.

Here is some really good news. The time of waiting is over! Hallelujah! Many people who focus on what the Disciples did as they waited are actually working to delay their own experience of the fire and baptism of the Holy Spirit. They are standing on the false belief that they have to do enough fasting, praying and decreeing to be worthy of it happening for them. It didn't happen then because of what the disciples did, and it will not happen now because of what you are doing. It is all about Yeshua ha Messiach and what He did. On the cross, he shouted, "It is finished!" It is a completed action. It is here, NOW! No more waiting! Just reach out by faith now and receive it in Yeshua's mighty name. Amen?

POWER TO WITNESS

The disciples needed power in order to effectively witness to all that Jesus had accomplished by His ministry, death, and resurrection. There was powerful opposition to this message, and they needed boldness to be able to speak out in the name of Yeshua. Jesus made it clear that this move of the Holy Spirit was coming to empower them to witness. Read the passage below and see how clearly He declared and decreed this to them and for them.

> *But you will receive power when the Holy Spirit comes on you; and you will be my witnesses in Jerusalem, and in all Judea and Samaria, and to the ends of the earth.* (Acts 1:8, NIV)

Soon after the outpouring of the Holy Spirit, this new movement of God became known as "The Way." Before the fledgling disciples got fully engaged in the power available in this move of the Lord, great hostility arose toward "the way." They were going through some really tough times of intense persecution. Many people today would simply abandon the Lord and seek protection from the opposition. This was not an option for them. They needed power, courage and boldness to accomplish their assigned mission. They were being called before councils, religious leaders and government authorities. We can learn some great lessons from their prayers during this time.

> *After they prayed, the place where they were meeting was shaken. And they were all filled with the Holy Spirit and spoke the word of God boldly. All the believers were one in heart and mind. No one claimed that any of his possessions was his own, but they shared everything they had. With great power the apostles continued to testify to the resurrection of the Lord Jesus, and much grace was upon them all.* (Acts 4:31-33, NIV)

They were being threatened with punishment and even death if they didn't stop using the name of Yeshua. Many of them were not only threatened, but were also beaten, stoned, imprisoned, and greatly despised. In spite of these things, they didn't ask to be hidden. That is not what they wanted. They wanted more boldness to witness, and they asked for healings, miracles, signs and wonders to accompany their preaching of the gospel of the Kingdom. The Lord gave a positive and powerful response to their prayers. Be careful when you ask for MORE! He will give it! When He releases this kind of power the ground still shakes, fire is still released, and boldness comes.

POWER OF UNITY

I think that most men like power tools whether they know how to use them or not. When we moved into our current home, it had no window dressing at all. We hung some sheets in the bedroom for the first night, but that was a temporary solution. We had company coming, and I needed to do something fast. We went to the hardware store and bought new blinds for the windows and installed them ourselves. When I got out my power screwdriver, I was disappointed. It didn't work and the battery would not take a charge. So, I began to install blinds with a common screwdriver. By the end of the day, the muscles in my arm cramped so badly that I could not let go of the screwdriver. I drove back to the hardware store and purchased a new electric screwdriver to finish the job. This is what I should have done from the beginning. I suddenly had a personal understanding of a scripture I had read many times.

Next to him was Eleazar son of Dodai the Ahohite. As one of the three mighty men,

> *he was with David when they taunted the Philistines gathered ‹at Pas Dammim› for battle. Then the men of Israel retreated, but he stood his ground and struck down the Philistines till his hand grew tired and froze to the sword.* (2 Samuel 23:9-10a, NIV)

I can truthfully say from personal experience that having a muscle cramp which freezes your hand to a tool or a weapon is very unpleasant and painful. Through this experience, I learned a great lesson on the value of power tools. I tend to look at everything as a potential word of prophecy. So, I sat down with my cramped arm to think this through. I realized that the Lord had a message for me in this painful lesson. He has some power tools for our work in the spiritual realm, but many of us are trying to do things manually with our own strength. Eventually our strength will wear out and our work will be halted until we get some new tools and learn how to use spiritual weapons. Perhaps David's man, Eleazar, needed an electric sword. Please excuse my use of this terminology. This is how my mind works.

> *For the weapons of our warfare are not carnal but mighty in God for pulling down strongholds, casting down arguments and every high thing that exalts itself against the knowledge of God, bringing every thought into captivity to the obedience of Christ, and being ready to punish all disobedience when your obedience is fulfilled.* (2 Corinthians 10:4-6)

As I reflected back on the situation with the disciples, I knew they needed some power tools to spread the gospel in the midst of so much persecution. They didn't need natural weapons like swords, spears and shields. They needed some spiritual power tools. They needed the power of unity. They needed to have their speech salted with the wisdom of the Holy Spirit. They needed the fire of God to come down once again and light the kindling in their spirits. The Lord answered their prayers and did all of these things for them on the Day of Pentecost.

> *When the Day of Pentecost had fully come, they were all with one accord in one place. And suddenly there came a sound from heaven, as of a rushing mighty wind, and it filled the whole house where they were sitting. Then there appeared to them divided tongues, as of fire, and one sat upon each of them. And they were all filled with the Holy Spirit and began to speak with other tongues, as the Spirit gave them utterance.* (Acts 2:1-4)

The Lord released some powerful lessons that day. He also inspired the writer to give some special spiritual lessons about power tools in this passage of scripture. I want to share three of these lessons with you. This was the first time they had ever been in one accord for anything. Something new had been released in them and for the Kingdom of God. The Lord gave them spiritual power through unity. Remember what Jesus taught in Matthew 18:19-20, "*Again I say to you that if two of you agree on earth concerning anything that they ask, it will be done for them by My Father in heaven. For where two or three are gathered together in My name, I am there in the midst of them.*" Their unity went beyond the natural. The risen Lord was in it with them, and His power was available to them.

They also received the power tool of language. Scholars have never fully agreed on what actually happened. Were they enabled to speak fluently in a number of different languages or did they speak some special language beyond the norm which was understandable to everyone present. I tend to believe the later explanation because they didn't seem to have to say the same thing over and over in different languages. This linguistic gift extended their unity beyond their small group and drew thousands of new believers into their fellowship. This was an amazing and powerful gift given for the purpose of growing the body of Christ so quickly.

There was also another level of unity experienced that day. For the first time they moved in complete unity with the Holy Spirit. Now that is power. I keep praying for the church to come back into unity glory. I pray that we will focus our energy on fighting the enemy instead of wasting so much time fighting with other believers. It is time to rekindle the Holy Spirit fires of unity in the church. I am praying for it, and I hope you will join with me in these prayers. Remember Paul's warning in Galatians 5:15 (NIV), "*If you keep on biting and devouring each other, watch out or you will be destroyed by each other.*"

NEW LEVEL OF DISCERNMENT

When this Holy Spirit fire came, it brought a new level of spiritual discernment to these Spirit-led believers. We also need a fresh anointing for spiritual discernment. It is very important to understand the times and the seasons of the Lord. We need to be more like the sons of Issachar (...*of the sons of Issachar who had understanding of the times, to know what Israel ought to do*, 1 Chronicles 12:32). The body of Christ needs this kind of wisdom and understanding to deal with the powerful spiritual struggles we face in these last days. Peter demonstrated this on the Day of Pentecost.

> *But Peter, standing up with the eleven, raised his voice and said to them, "Men of Judea and all who dwell in Jerusalem, let this be known to you, and heed my words. For these are not drunk, as you suppose, since it is only the third hour of the day. But this is what was spoken by the prophet Joel: 'And it shall come to pass in the last days, says God, That I will pour out of My Spirit on all flesh; Your sons and your daughters shall prophesy, Your young men shall see visions, Your old men shall dream dreams. And on My men-servants and on My maidservants I will pour out My Spirit in those days; And they shall prophesy. I will show wonders in heaven above and signs in the earth beneath: Blood and fire and vapor of smoke. The sun shall be turned into darkness, and the moon into blood, before the coming of the great and awesome day of the Lord. And it shall come to pass that whoever calls on the name of the Lord Shall be saved.'"* (Acts 2:14-21)

I have heard many messages which claimed that what people saw and what Peter described were two very different sets of facts. They claimed that the people didn't see the fulfillment of Joel's prophecy in a literal sense, but in a spiritual sense. The main issue was about the sun turning dark and the moon looking like blood. The interesting thing is that we seem to have new information now.

We know from the scriptures that the sun became dark as Jesus died on the cross. The new information is that there was a blood moon on that Passover night. Now the disciples were manifesting a new level of prophetic utterance and they fully understood the signs of the times. The Holy Spirit gave Peter a new level of spiritual discernment so that he could see the full meaning of what happened on that observance of Shavuot. Peter and the other disciples now fully understood that they were living in the last days.

WE NEED MORE OF THIS
FIRE AND POWER

I am experiencing an increased spiritual hunger and thirst for more of this Holy Spirit power. How about you? I am constantly asking the Lord for more fire. Knowing that the disciples received more than one infilling of the Holy Spirit, I am encouraged to seek more for myself and more for you. It is time for a fresh impartation of fire and power! Do you agree? Remember if we ask in agreement, it brings the presence and power of the risen Savior into our midst.

I am releasing an impartation to you right now for more fire and more power. Just lift your hands to the Lord and receive it. This too is scriptural. Remember what Paul declared in Romans 1:11, "*For I long to see you, that I may impart to you some spiritual gift, so that you may be established...*" These things are spiritual gifts and are subject to impartation. So once again I release the impartation of fire and power to you! When you receive it, release it to others in the body of Christ. Remember what Jesus said in Matthew 10:8, "*Freely you have received, freely give.*"

When we receive and then impart the fire and power of the Lord, perhaps we will see the fires of revival break out again. We have been called to prepare the way for the Lord's return. We need fire and power to bring in the harvest today. I am ready for another harvest like they experienced in the days following the outpouring of the Holy Spirit and fire. How about you? Now is the time to ask, seek, and knock. The Lord is waiting for faithful disciples to arise and be ready to move with power and fire. Will you be one?

PRAYER

Grace to you and peace from God our Father and the Lord Jesus Christ. We give thanks to the God and Father of our Lord Jesus Christ, praying always for you, since we heard of your faith in Christ Jesus and of your love for all the saints; because of the hope which is laid up for you in heaven, of which you heard before in the word of the truth of the gospel, which has come to you, as it has also in all the world, and is bringing forth fruit, as it is also among you since the day you heard and knew the grace of God in truth; as you also learned from Epaphras, our dear fellow servant, who is a faithful minister of Christ on your behalf, who also declared to us your love in the Spirit. For this reason we also, since the day we heard it, do not cease to pray for you, and to ask that you may be filled with the knowledge of His will in all wisdom and spiritual understanding; that you may walk worthy of the Lord, fully pleasing Him, being fruitful in every good work and increasing in the knowledge of God; strengthened with all might, according to His glorious power, for all patience and longsuffering with joy; giving thanks to the Father who has qualified us to be partakers of the inheritance of the saints in the light. He has delivered us from the power of darkness and conveyed us into the kingdom of the Son of His love, in whom we have redemption through His blood, the for-giveness of sins. (Colossians 1:2b-14)

PAUSE AND REFLECT

1. What are the three basic elements of power in the natural universe?

2. How do the scriptures use these elements to describe the Holy Spirit?

3. Why did Jesus tell the disciples to wait in Jerusalem?

4. What was the specific purpose for the power they were to receive?

5. Why is unity so important for us?

6. How can you receive a fresh anointing for greater spiritual discernment?

CHAPTER FIVE

REFINED IN THE FIRE

Gold, silver, bronze, iron, tin, lead and any-thing else that can withstand fire must be put through the fire, and then it will be clean. But it must also be purified with the water of cleansing. And whatever cannot withstand fire must be put through that water. (Numbers 31:22-23, NIV)

I want to remind you that fire is mentioned in the Bible at least 503 times! It must be important if God's Word brings it up that many times! Ask yourself how many sermons have you heard or preached on the fire of God? By comparison, prayer is only mentioned 129. Think about it. Fire is mentioned in the Bible almost four times as often as prayer. You may be wondering why I am repeating this information. I am bringing this up again because there is another word mentioned as often as fire. That word is love. Love is also mentioned 503 times.

Going through this process of comparison led me to meditate on the relationship between these two con-cepts. I came to a strong conclusion which you may not immediately accept. I believe there is a strong connection between the love of God and the fire of God. If you are doubtful, I ask you to reserve judgment until we go through this idea together. Keep this question in your mind as we work through these ideas together.

The main connection I saw between these two powerful words is that God can only trust you with as much fire as your love can handle without hurting someone. People who are spiritually immature can do more harm than good if they receive power without love. We often see this as people begin to move in the prophetic anointing. They tell everything as soon as they hear it. This can cause conflict and hurt in families, friendships and churches.

It takes time for people to mature in their gifting. Gradually, they learn to wait for the right moment and the right place to release a prophetic word. Newly gifted people need to learn to wait for words of wisdom from the Holy Spirit. You need the wisdom given in order to properly handle many of the prophetic messages from the Lord. We previously looked at Luke 9:52-56. It was the account of James and John wanting to bring the fire of God on people who did not welcome Jesus. They were still immature disciples who needed more discipline from the Lord. Jesus provided them with additional training in the use of the power gifts of the Spirit. In John's first letter, it is clear that he had learned the lessons for the use of love in ministry.

The Disciples wanted to destroy people with the fire of God. They seemed to have the attitude: If you don't welcome me, I'll call down fire on you. Do you know anyone who responds like that? Angry, hurting people often angrily hurt other people. This rule applies to us as well. Angry Christians may also hurt people. When an angry and unforgiving person gets saved, they are angry and unforgiving Christians. They need time with the Lord to work on their character defects in order to rise above their emotions. It doesn't often happen immediately. People need to grow and mature in love so that the Lord can release the power gifts to them. This is why Paul taught us to pursue love before we seek spiritual gifts. 1 Corinthians 14:1, "*Pursue love, and desire spiritual gifts, but especially that you may prophesy.*"

As you mature in the Word of God, you begin to see how the Lord feels and thinks about certain character traits. Consider the ones listed below. If you have any of these traits (and most of us have some degree of these still remaining in our hearts), perhaps it is time to return to Paul's prophetic prime directive and once again "pursue love." As you study these, remember the message in Proverbs 6:16-19, "*These six things the Lord hates, yes, seven are an abomination to Him: a proud look, a lying tongue, hands that shed innocent blood, a heart that devises wicked plans, feet that are swift in running to evil, a false witness who speaks lies, and one who sows discord among brethren.* I don't want to do the things the Lord hates. I want to avoid the things which are an abomination to Him. How about you?

1. Verbal abuse: how does God feel about it?

   The tongue also is a fire, a world of evil among the parts of the body. It corrupts the whole body, sets the whole course of one's life on fire, and is itself set on fire by hell. (James 3:6, NIV)

2. Physical abuse: How does God feel about it? He commands us to love one another.

By this everyone will know that you are my disciples, if you love one another. (John 13:35, NIV)

3. The victims of abuse are God's own children. When they are hurt by others, it upsets Him.

For this is what the LORD Almighty says: "After the Glorious One has sent me against the nations that have plundered you—for whoever touches you touches the apple of his eye." (Zechariah 2:8, NIV)

IF YOU WANT THE FIRE OF GOD LET LOVE RULE YOUR HEART!

Follow the way of love and eagerly desire gifts of the Spirit, especially prophecy. (1 Corinthians 14:1, NIV)

If you have been hurt by someone in the past, take it to God for healing. If someone has refused to forgive you, give it over to the Lord. If someone has decided to be your enemy and use you in spiteful ways, remember what Jesus said in Luke 6:27-28, *"But I say to you who hear: Love your enemies, do good to those who hate you, bless those who curse you, and pray for those who spitefully use you."* Jesus set a very high standard for those who would follow Him. We must rise to the challenge and let everything be tendered with His love.

We must not get caught up in making accusations about other believers. As you have been taught by the Scriptures, remember who accuses your brothers and sisters in the faith. I don't want to be doing the work of the "accuser of the brethren (Revelation 12:10)." I am a servant of Yeshua ha Messiach and I want to do His will and accomplish His purposes. How about you? If this is also your choice, then make a decision today to bless and not curse. Don't let your hurt cause you to sin.

> *In all this you greatly rejoice, though now for a little while you may have had to suffer grief in all kinds of trials. These have come so that the proven genuineness of your faith— of greater worth than gold, which perishes even though refined by fire —may result in praise, glory and honor when Jesus Christ is revealed.* (1 Peter 1:6-7, NIV)

It is time to let the fire of God refine our faith and our hearts so that we can prove that we are genuinely connected to Yeshua. Don't let your emotions put out your fire. Let the fire of God in your heart extinguish the flames of all these negative emotions. Remember Paul's teaching in 1 Thessalonians 5:19-20 (NIV), "*Do not put out the Spirit's fire; do not treat prophecies with contempt.*" Let your focus be on helping Jesus accomplish His goal. Remember what He declared in Luke 12:49 (NIV), "*I have come to bring fire on the earth, and how I wish it were already kindled!*" Carry the fire, but use it with the love of God.

Let your desire be for the fire of God to refine your spirit. We need to do this now while there is still time. A time is coming when it will be too late to change. A time is coming when we will stand before the judgment seat of Christ and account for the things we have done. When that time comes, I want to be ready to let Him know that I learned to love as He loves. I want to be ready to testify that I used His gifts to bless others rather than to curse them. I want Him to know that I allowed the Holy Spirit to bring fire into my heart to refine and purify it. How about you? Remember the warning released in Malachi 3:2, "*But who can endure the day of his coming? Who can stand when he appears? For he will be like a refiner's fire or a launderer's soap.*" The one who has already been through the fire will endure that day.

Fire burns and most people want to avoid the fire, but the righteous choice has been made clear. We can let fire purify us now or fail the test later and only then discover that we are unable to stand before Him in that day. I am crying out for the fire of God to come now and do its work. How about you? Are you seeking the fire of God to refine and purify your heart to prepare you for the season of His return? Most of us need to cry out like Isaiah. We are people of unclean lips. How can we speak the pure and holy Word of God with these lips and this tongue? It is time to let Him make us ready so that we can answer the Lord's calling.

> *So I said: "Woe is me, for I am undone! Because I am a man of unclean lips, and I dwell in the midst of a people of unclean lips; for my eyes have seen the King, The Lord of hosts." Then one of the seraphim flew to me, having in his hand a live coal which he had taken with the tongs from the altar. And he touched my mouth with it, and said: "Behold, this has touched your lips; your iniquity is taken away, and your sin purged."* (Isaiah 6:5-7)

I want you to receive all the promises of God. That is why I am writing this book and releasing these teachings.

My heart aches for you and for me to come closer to the Lord and be made ready to serve Him in this hour. Remember what the Lord declared in Jeremiah 23:29, *"Is not my word like fire," declares the Lord, "and like a hammer that breaks a rock in pieces*?" How can we handle the Word of God unless we allow Him to burn away the things which cannot endure the fire? We must do this so that the other parts of our character can move with Him. Meditate on what the Lord said to the prophet Zechariah. *"This third I will bring into the fire; I will refine them like silver and test them like gold. They will call on my name and I will answer them; I will say, They are my people, and they will say, The Lord is our God."* (Zechariah 13:9, NIV) The refining fire makes it possible for us to know the Lord as our Lord and Savior. Amen?

We have to endure the fire to be able to carry the fire of God. The Lord is still looking for people who are ready to carry the fire of revival in these last days. He is still seeking those willing to be transformed so they can do His work and release His love into a sick and dying world. People are not truly ready until they have been through the fire. Servants are not prepared until they are refined and purified. Sometimes we must release a word about a coming judgment. The Lord doesn't want us to speak these things out of our own anger. Remember: You cannot receive an anointing like the Lord gave to Jeremiah until you have been prepared. Study the passage below and ask the Lord to prepare your heart and your mind.

> *Therefore this is what the Lord God Almighty says: "Because the people have spoken these words, I will make my words in your mouth a fire and these people the wood it consumes."* (Jeremiah 5:14, NIV)

110

With this anointing of fire, many believers would respond like James and John in the passage you studied earlier. They would be calling down the fire of God to destroy the people who didn't agree with them or who didn't see things exactly like they do. If you are on Facebook, you know what I mean. Some people who claim to be believers spew out judgment and condemnation on others in angry and merciless ways. Remember the lesson given in Numbers 26:61 (NIV), "*But Nadab and Abihu died when they made an offering before the LORD with unauthorized fire.*"

When we spew out venom on other believers or even unbelievers, we are releasing unauthorized fire. We must not allow this to happen. We must not be like the people Jeremiah described in Jeremiah 6:29, (NIV), "*The bellows blow fiercely to burn away the lead with fire, but the refining goes on in vain; the wicked are not purged out.*" Only the wicked refuse the refining fire of the Lord which purges out sin.

We do not work for the "accuser of the brethren." We work for the God who is love. We have chosen to bless and not to curse. When we begin to make our pursuit of love with more intensity than we use in seeking spiritual gifts, we are beginning to get closer to what the Lord has called us to do. When every word is released with love and with an intent to build up, strengthen and comfort the Lord's people, He can begin to trust us with the fire. When that time comes, you will know it. You will feel something of what Jeremiah described in Jeremiah 20:9, "*Then I said, 'I will not make mention of Him, nor speak anymore in His name.' But His word was in my heart like a burning fire shut up in my bones; I was weary of holding it back, and I could not.*

There is a powerful promise given to those who belong to the Lord. I want to receive everything He promised. How about you? For those who are willing to move toward the Lord in faith and allow Him to do His mighty work in them, He has promised to be with them and to protect them from all harm. This is the good news. If you are still afraid of the fire, take hold of this promise. Let the Lord make you fireproof. Receive His promise that the fire will do you no harm.

> *When you pass through the waters, I will be with you; and when you pass through the rivers, they will not sweep over you. When you walk through the fire, you will not be burned; the flames will not set you ablaze.* (Isaiah 43:2)

You don't need to fear His fire, and you certainly do not need to fear the fire of the enemy. You do not need to fear the fiery words of those who still move in the flesh and not in the Spirit. Embrace the promise in the passage above. Read it over and over. Read it aloud. Read it until it becomes your faith and the source of your testimony.

Vision Report
Jesus showed me a calendar in heaven

This morning the Lord began to show me faces in heaven which would normally be viewed as unlovely. I had the same experience yesterday with a different set of faces, but something was different today. As I looked at the faces, I could see them as Jesus saw them, and they were beautiful indeed. Some tried to make frowning faces or mean looking faces. It didn't matter, Jesus loved them anyway, and I was feeling that love. I wanted to heal their hurts, calm their rage, reverse the damage of time and just bring total restoration to them.

Jesus' promise about this two week period of ministry in Korea has been coming true more and more each day. We are starting each conference/revival at the level you normally expect to end the meetings. Then the next meeting gets even more intense. The intensity continues to rise higher and higher each day. Each day I feel more energized and more on fire for Jesus. More on fire by the Holy Spirit. More in love with Father God every day! Hallelujah!

This morning, I asked the Lord about His plan for today. In June, He pointed out that this day would be the high point of our ministry trip, but He did not say what was going to happen. He told me that after today, we would stay at that level for 10 more days. I wanted to know what to expect today. So I asked. The Lord said that the great outpouring for today will be an abundance of the love of the Father. Today, we will be able to experience His love in our hearts more than we have every felt it before. Today, The Lord is pouring it out as never before. Are you ready to receive it?

In the past, I have experienced that outpouring three different times and it was so overwhelming and wonderful. I felt like the Lord had poured some kind of great and heavy anointing of love into me for other people. I have never looked at people the same way since that experience. When I look at people, I just want to tell them how much God loves them. I try so hard and I'm not sure if they really get it. His love is so much greater than we have ever been told, greater than we have ever experienced, and we are being allowed to feel it more clearly now than we have ever felt it before.

Open up today to receive an outpouring of His overwhelming love. Feel it for yourself and then immediately stop looking at yourself and feel it for others. Let the Lord pour more and more of His amazing and wonderful love into you today and then pass it on to those around you. From now on, see everyone and everything differently as if you are seeing them through His eyes and with His heart. Begin to see and feel from an eternal perspective. That is the mighty outpouring for today. It is to love others as much as you love yourself. To begin to seek anointing and impartation for them as you have sought if for yourself. It is time to take your eyes off of self and focus on others.

I don't think we have grasped the depth of the Biblical idea that "God is love!" I don't think we have felt it in the profound way He wants us to feel it today. It is time to stop looking so much to ourselves with all our desires and needs, and to see clearly what we can give to others. When we fully move in this anointing, we will live in the fulfillment of the words of Jesus in John 13:35, *"By this all will know that you are My disciples, if you have love for one another."*

This outpouring is for a level of love to rise up in your heart which is so powerful that others will quickly see it and feel it. They will see it in you, and be drawn to you to receive more. They will see Jesus living in you and be drawn to receive more of the Father's love. When you allow the Lord to do this, you will experience for yourself more of what Peter meant in 1 Peter 4:8, *"And above all things have fervent love for one another, for love will cover a multitude of sins."* When this love comes upon you, it will literally cover over everything from your past and make all things new in your life. It will also cover over everything in the past of those you are seeing and loving through His eyes.

114

(End of Vision Report)
PRAYER

Oh! How I am praying for you today. I want you to receive the fullness of the Father's love. I want you to be filled with it! I want you to be changed by it. I want you to become the living Word of God through the overwhelming love you begin to shed into the lives of others. May you stand under an open heaven today! May you receive the downpour! May it fill you! May He press it down, shake it together, and keep it overflowing in and through you! Amen and Amen! Hallelujah! Thank you Jesus for the extreme gift of love today! Amen and Amen! Hallelujah, Jesus! Thank you Father God! Thank you Holy Spirit!

Search me, O God, and know my heart; try me, and know my anxieties; and see if there is any wicked way in me, and lead me in the way everlasting. (Psalm 139:23-24)

RECEIVE THE PROMISE

For thus says the LORD: After seventy years are completed at Babylon, I will visit you and perform My good word toward you, and cause you to return to this place. For I know the thoughts that I think toward you, says the LORD, thoughts of peace and not of evil, to give you a future and a hope. Then you will call upon Me and go and pray to Me, and I will listen to you. And you will seek Me and find Me, when you search for Me with all your heart. (Jeremiah 29:10-13)

PAUSE AND REFLECT

1. Which word is mentioned in the Bible the same number of times as fire?

2. Is there a connection between these two powerful words? If so, what is it?

3. Why do you think people try to avoid the fire of God?

4. Why does the Lord want us to pursue love before spiritual gifts?

5. How can you be refined, purified and made ready for service?

6. How does the Lord make you fireproof?

CHAPTER SIX

OUTCOMES OF HOLY SPIRIT FIRE

VISION REPORT
ASIAN FAN OF FIRE

This morning, the Lord gave me an awesome vision of an open heaven. I love to see and experience the Open Heaven. Each time I see it, I am filled with wonder and awe as powerfully as the first time. The things of God and His power and glory never get old and never lose their aura of amazement for me. It was like that this morning during my visit to Heaven. I am praying for you to have many experiences like this so that you can also be caught up in the wonder and awe of the Lord.

As I looked intently into the opening into Heaven, I was filled with great expectation. As often happens, it didn't manifest the way I expected. The Lord is always doing new things. Remember what He said in Revelation 21:5, *"Then He who sat on the throne said, 'Behold, I make all things new.' And He said to me, 'Write, for these words are true and faithful.'"* The Lord always gives above and beyond all we ask or imagine. Read aloud Ephesians

3:20-21, *"Now to Him who is able to do exceedingly abundantly above all that we ask or think, according to the power that works in us, to Him be glory in the church by Christ Jesus to all generations, forever and ever. Amen."* This morning He did not disappoint me or provide less than this promise.

As I tried to press in through the open portal into Heaven, something was holding me back. I didn't understand it at first and continued to press in to move through the opening. Then suddenly, an awesome release of His glory poured out through the opening toward earth. I had been held back so that I could see and experience what the Lord was doing. This outpouring of His glory looked like liquid fire. It was amber in color and seemed to be blazing with the power of God. As it descended, it began to take on a different shape. It began to look like a giant Asian fan being thrown open high over the earth. Like the previous flow of His glory, the fan looked like blazing fire with a radiant amber color.

I was suddenly aware that all of this was being poured out toward everyone willing to receive it. Those unwilling to receive it will not even be aware of its presence. I felt a deep sadness for those who are not open to receiving from the glory of the Lord. I prayed for Spirit-filled people to open their spiritual eyes to see, their spiritual ears to hear, and their spiritual hearts to perceive what the Lord is doing in this hour. I remembered what Moses told the people in his generation. As you read the passage below, think about how sad this was for them, and how sad it will be for those in this generation who still cannot receive the spiritual things of the Lord.

Now Moses called all Israel and said to them:
You have seen all that the LORD did before

*your eyes in the land of Egypt, to Pharaoh
and to all his servants and to all his land—
the great trials which your eyes have seen,
the signs, and those great wonders. Yet the
LORD has not given you a heart to perceive
and eyes to see and ears to hear, to this very
day. And I have led you forty years in the
wilderness. Your clothes have not worn out
on you, and your sandals have not worn out
on your feet. You have not eaten bread, nor
have you drunk wine or similar drink, that
you may know that I am the LORD your God.*
(Deuteronomy 29:2-6)

As I thought about sharing this experience with you,
the Lord said, "Many people do not understand what you
are talking about when you speak of an open heaven,
because they have not yet seen it or experienced it. Don't
be surprised that they don't understand your words. Pray
for their eyes to be opened to see all that the Father has
for them and that their ears will be opened to hear what
He is saying to them today." So, I am praying today for
your eyes, ears and hearts to be open to see and receive
all the Lord is pouring out to you in order to help you
accomplish your purpose in the Kingdom. Amen!

(End of Vision Report)
FIRE OF THE HOLY SPIRIT

*Then I looked, and behold, a whirlwind was
coming out of the north, a great cloud with
raging fire engulfing itself; and brightness
was all around it and radiating out of its midst
like the color of amber, out of the midst of*

the fire. Also from within it came the likeness of four living creatures. And this was their appearance: they had the likeness of a man. Each one had four faces, and each one had four wings. Their legs were straight, and the soles of their feet were like the soles of calves' feet. They sparkled like the color of burnished bronze. The hands of a man were under their wings on their four sides; and each of the four had faces and wings. Their wings touched one another. The creatures did not turn when they went, but each one went straight forward. (Ezekiel 1:4-9)

Many of the accounts of the Lord's fire are filled with strange imagery and can seem almost surreal. It is difficult for many people to visualize this scene. As a result, they often just gloss over passages like the one above without seeking the Lord's wisdom to understand it. I am convinced that in this season the Lord is calling us to look again at the fire, and to seek an ever deepening understanding of the mystery of His glory in the fire. As John the Baptizer came on the scene to announce the coming of Messiach, he made an unusual proclamation about what would happen.

Now as the people were in expectation, and all reasoned in their hearts about John, whether he was the Christ or not, John answered, saying to all, "I indeed baptize you with water; but One mightier than I is coming, whose sandal strap I am not worthy to loose. He will baptize you with the Holy Spirit and fire. His winnowing fan is in His hand, and

*He will thoroughly clean out His threshing
floor, and gather the wheat into His barn; but
the chaff He will burn with unquenchable fire."*
(Luke 3:15-17)

Most people, then and now, understand the baptism
of water. This cleansing ritual was practiced for generations in the Hebrew culture. Many of us have grown up
fully aware of this baptism with water. It is a little more
challenging to understand the baptism of the Holy Spirit.
Even some Jewish leaders like Nicodemus struggled to
understand the new birth and the baptism of the Holy
Spirit. It didn't become fully understood until after the Day
of Pentecost. But what about this baptism of fire? How
many really understood it when John proclaimed it? How
many understand it today.

*I still have many things to say to you, but you
cannot bear them now. However, when He,
the Spirit of truth, has come, He will guide
you into all truth; for He will not speak on His
own authority, but whatever He hears He will
speak; and He will tell you things to come. He
will glorify Me, for He will take of what is Mine
and declare it to you.* (John 16:12-14)

There are many things about the Kingdom of God which
natural wisdom cannot comprehend. Natural wisdom
brings very little revelation concerning the things of the
Spirit. As with those first followers of Yeshua, we need
for the Spirit of truth and the Spirit of wisdom and revelation to minister this understanding to us today. I have
prayed for a long time to receive this wisdom from the
Holy Spirit. I have diligently pursued this understanding,

and I am convinced there is only one way to get it. It works the same way now as it did then. You need for Jesus to breathe on you and release the Spirit of truth to work with you and in you.

> *So Jesus said to them again, "Peace to you! As the Father has sent Me, I also send you." And when He had said this, He breathed on them, and said to them, "Receive the Holy Spirit.* (John 20:21-22)

Ask the Lord to breathe this same gift on you. In meetings I have often breathed into the microphone as a means of breathing over the people. I do this as an impartation and release of the Spirit. I do this because I believe what Jesus taught in John Chapter Fourteen. We have been given an anointing to do what He did and release what He released. As His disciples, we can impart as He imparted. As you read the passage below claim it once more for yourself. Claim it with great faith and great authority so that you can walk in the great grace it still releases to His disciples today.

> *Most assuredly, I say to you, he who believes in Me, the works that I do he will do also; and greater works than these he will do, because I go to My Father. And whatever you ask in My name, that I will do, that the Father may be glorified in the Son. If you ask anything in My name, I will do it.* (John 14:12-14)

After Jesus breathed on them and released this anointing of the Holy Spirit, He taught them the advanced things of the kingdom of God for forty days. All of this happened following His resurrection. I want to know and understand these advanced things of the Kingdom. How about you? Then pause right now and breathe the Spirit of truth into your own heart and soul. Edwin Hatch understood much about this when he penned the words of one of the all-time best loved hymns, "Breathe on Me Breath of God." Read the lyrics slowly and deeply as you let the revelation begin:

Breathe on me, Breath of God,
Fill me with life anew,
That I may love what Thou dost love,
And do what Thou wouldst do.
Breathe on me, Breath of God,
Until my heart is pure,
Until with Thee I will one will,
To do and to endure.
Breathe on me, Breath of God,
Till I am wholly Thine,
Until this earthly part of me
Glows with Thy fire divine.
Breathe on me, Breath of God,
So shall I never die,
But live with Thee the perfect life
Of Thine eternity.
(Edwin Hatch, 1878, Public Domain)

May you also receive the fullness of this outpouring of the Holy Spirit and fire! May you be filled the way Edwin Hatch prayed: *"Until this earthly part of me glows with Thy fire divine."* As you contemplate these things you may be asking the same question as so many in the past have asked: If I receive this baptism of fire, what will the outcomes be for me? How will it change my life and my ministry? What will it cost? Will I be willing and able to pay the price? In the sections below, I will present several of these spiritual outcomes. Some of these outcomes are explained in greater detail in other sections of this book. I put them together here to assist you in organizing your thoughts for this study. I will also continue to pray for the Spirit of truth to guide you into even more truth than I received in writing this.

A FIRE WHICH BRINGS FREEDOM

> *Therefore, because the king's command was urgent, and the furnace exceedingly hot, the flame of the fire killed those men who took up Shadrach, Meshach, and Abedn-Nego. And these three men, Shadrach, Meshach, and Abed-Nego, fell down bound into the midst of the burning fiery furnace. Then King Nebuchadnezzar was astonished; and he rose in haste and spoke, saying to his counselors, "Did we not cast three men bound into the midst of the fire?" They answered and said to the king, "True, O king." "Look!" he answered, "I see four men loose, walking in the midst of the fire; and they are not hurt, and the form of the fourth is like the Son of God."* (Daniel 3:22-25)

The story of Shadrach, Meshach, and Abed-Nego in the fiery furnace tells us a great deal about our trust in the Lord, His mastery over fire, and His presence in it. Do you trust the Lord enough to go into the fire rather than to deny Him? In the quiet times of meditation, we bravely say we will do it, but like Peter standing by the fire in the

High Priest's courtyard we may not be so brave. Trust is something we need to develop before the fire comes. That is what these three men did in their time. Because they had known His power, love and grace, they could stand against all the king's threats of a terrible death.

> *Shadrach, Meshach, and Abed-Nego answered and said to the king, "O Nebuchadnezzar, we have no need to answer you in this matter. If that is the case, our God whom we serve is able to deliver us from the burning fiery furnace, and He will deliver us from your hand, O king. But if not, let it be known to you, O king, that we do not serve your gods, nor will we worship the gold image which you have set up."* (Daniel 3:16-18)

You need to rehearse often all the benefits of the Lord which have been released in your life and ministry by faith. Speak them aloud over and over. Build up your faith so that when the test comes the fire will be as inconsequential as those other small obstacles which have been overcome by faith in the past. *"But you, beloved, building yourselves up on your most holy faith, praying in the Holy Spirit, keep yourselves in the love of God, looking for the mercy of our Lord Jesus Christ unto eternal life."* Jude 1:20-21) How do you build up your faith? Remember what Paul taught in Romans 10:17, *"So then faith comes by hearing, and hearing by the word of God."* Let the words of these three faithful men be spoken through your lips often so that your faith will be greater than all the fiery furnaces of this world.

ONLY THEIR BONDS WERE BURNED

Then Nebuchadnezzar went near the mouth of the burning fiery furnace and spoke, saying, "Shadrach, Meshach, and Abed-Nego, servants of the Most High God, come out, and come here." Then Shadrach, Meshach, and Abed-Nego came from the midst of the fire. And the satraps, administrators, governors, and the king's counselors gathered together, and they saw these men on whose bodies the fire had no power; the hair of their head was not singed nor were their garments affected, and the smell of fire was not on them. (Daniel 3:26-27)

What comes out of the "fire?" Freedom is the end product of the fiery trials you must face in your walk with the Lord! As you go from one of these trials to another, your faith becomes stronger than the bonds placed on you by the world. You get set free from your two greatest enemies: fear and death! The fire of King Nebuchadnezzar had no effect on them at all. It wasn't able to burn any part of their physical being. It wasn't able to burn their clothing. Not even the smell of the fire could stick to them in the presence of the Son of God. The one thing it did was to burn away the things which bound them. They were set free both physically and spiritually in the fire. This same Lord and savior is with you in your fiery trials. Amen?

NO BONDAGE TO FEAR

These men were unafraid before they were cast into the fire because of their faith. Can you imagine the new level of their faith after the fire? They were set free from the physical bonds used to restrain them before the fire, and they were free from the bonds of all fear in the future. That is also the Lord's plan for your life. As you read this aloud over and over, you will build up that faith in your own heart. Decree it aloud right now: I am no longer in bondage to fear! Keep saying it until you know it in the depth of your heart. Remember: there is no reward for cowardly behavior. Even in worldly literature, there are no great stories about the exploits of cowards. In the Bible, we see the final outcome for those who are in bondage to fear and act as cowards.

> *But the cowardly, the unbelieving, the vile, the murderers, the sexually immoral, those who practice magic arts, the idolaters and all liars—their place will be in the fiery lake of burning sulfur. This is the second death.* (Revelation 21:8, NIV)

NO BONDAGE TO DECEPTION

> *But Jesus called them to Himself and said, "You know that the rulers of the Gentiles lord it over them, and those who are great exercise authority over them. Yet it shall not be so among you; but whoever desires to become great among you, let him be your servant. And whoever desires to be first among you, let him be your slave—just as the Son of Man did not come to be served, but to serve, and to give His life a ransom for many."* (Matthew 20:25-28)

Those who are leaders in the world seek to keep people in bondage so they can stay in control. It has always been like that in the natural, but it is not to be like that in the spiritual realm. We have been set free from doubt and hopelessness. Decree over and over: I am not in bondage to doubt! I am not in bondage to fear! I have been set free through the gift of faith. It is true. You have been set free. Hallelujah! You are now free to serve the Lord out of respect, love and faith. You are free to be elevated in your anointing. You are made ready to do the *"greater things"* the Lord spoke about in John 14:12. Receive all this by faith right now. Amen?

FIRE WHICH PURIFIES THE BODY

I baptize you with water for repentance. But after me will come one who is more powerful than I, whose sandals I am not fit to carry. He will baptize you with the Holy Spirit and with fire. His winnowing fork is in his hand, and he will clear his threshing floor, gathering his wheat into the barn and burning up the chaff with unquenchable fire. (Matthew 3:11-12)

When these words were first declared, the people were looking forward in hope for this to manifest. It is different for you. You have already received it. John spoke of *"one who is more powerful,"* but he hadn't seen him yet. He was operating out of faith in the Word of God. You are so blessed, because you have seen Him. He has been made visible to you in the Word of God and by the testimony of the Holy Spirit. Yeshua is that one who was promised to come and baptize with the Holy Spirit and with fire. Do you know Him? It is so important to know Him. Seek it with all your heart. You can't do it without Him. If you don't know Him or if you are uncertain, take care of that shortcoming right now. Confess Him as your Lord and Savior. Open your heart and let Him enter to reign in your life. Let Him baptize you right now. Amen?

Yeshua ha Messiach has fulfilled all that John prophesied. If you have submitted to Him as Lord, He has fulfilled it in you. He has baptized you. He has gathered you in like a farmer gathers wheat into the barn. He has conveyed you into the "kingdom of the Son of His love." He has covered you with eternal life which cannot be taken away from you. You are His and He is yours forever. Amen? He has also burned the chaff of sin out of your life with unquenchable fire. One day all those who have received Him will face another fire and many will be burned.

> *Then I heard him call out in a loud voice, "Bring the guards of the city here, each with a weapon in his hand." And I saw six men coming from the direction of the upper gate, which faces north, each with a deadly weapon in his hand. With them was a man clothed in linen who had a writing kit at his side. They came in and stood beside the bronze altar. Now the glory of the God of Israel went up from above the cherubim, where it had been, and moved to the threshold of the temple. Then the Lord called to the man clothed in linen who had the writing kit at his side and said to him, "Go throughout the city of Jerusalem and put a mark on the foreheads of those who grieve and lament over all the detestable things that are done in it." (Ezekiel 9:1-6, NIV)*

HAVE YOU RECEIVED THE MARK?

If you have been baptized with the Holy Spirit and with fire, then you have received the mark of God! You are marked as one who has already gone thru the FIRE! You have also been marked as one who carries the FIRE of God. You have been marked for eternal life. I love to pray the Aaronic Blessing over and over. I pray it every day. How about you?

> *And the Lord spoke to Moses, saying: "Speak to Aaron and his sons, saying, 'This is the way you shall bless the children of Israel. Say to them: "The Lord bless you and keep you; the Lord make His face shine upon you, and be gracious to you; the Lord lift up His countenance upon you, and give you peace."'"*
> (Numbers 6:22-26)

Think about it! The result of this blessing is to have the name of God placed on you (Numbers 6:27, *"So they shall put My name on the children of Israel, and I will bless them."*) Decree it aloud: I have the name of the Lord on me. I have been marked for all eternity as one of His sheep. I am marked as one of His people. I have the mark of a true disciple of Yeshua ha Messiach. Amen!

A FIRE THAT BRINGS POWER

> *When the day of Pentecost came, they were all together in one place. Suddenly a sound like the blowing of a violent wind came from heaven and filled the whole house where they were sitting. They saw what seemed to*

be tongues of fire that separated and came to rest on each of them. All of them were filled with the Holy Spirit and began to speak in other tongues as the Spirit enabled them. (Acts 2:1-4, NIV)

WHEN FIRE FALLS

Some people read the passage above and only receive it as an account of something which happened in the past for these few individuals. Others read it and claim it for themselves. They accept it by faith and participate in it with disciples throughout the centuries. I am like this second type. I believe that every promise in the Bible is for me. I also believe that every promise is for you if you believe in Yeshua ha Messiach. If they received the fire of the Holy Spirit, then it is available for you and me. Amen?

The things which happened on that first Day of Pentecost were only the beginning. They were like some of the birth pangs of the Kingdom of God which Jesus spoke about. If you agree, then make a decree: The out-pouring which began at Pentecost has only started. Now, it is coming into its fullness. Are you ready? Keep believing and continue receiving. Say with me: if it was for them, it is also for me. I receive it by faith in the name of Yeshua ha Messiach.

After the disciples' second experience with the out-pouring of a Holy Spirit baptism, it is recorded in Acts 4:33, *"And with great power the apostles gave witness to the resurrection of the Lord Jesus. And great grace was upon them all."* Jesus told them that they would receive power, but I don't think they fully understood how much. I don't think they knew that they could keep receiving more and more. How about you? Have you received the power?

Have you been receiving more and more? It is time to open up your receivers and cry out in faith for more power, more Holy Spirit fire and more faith. I do this often. I want more Holy Spirit fire and power. I want to have the "great grace" which was on all of them. How about you? Then begin to press in for it right now.

A FIRE TO BRING US TO FULLNESS

And it shall come to pass afterward that I will pour out My Spirit on all flesh; your sons and your daughters shall prophesy, your old men shall dream dreams, your young men shall see visions. And also on My menservants and on My maidservants I will pour out My Spirit in those days. And I will show wonders in the heavens and in the earth: blood and fire and pillars of smoke. The sun shall be turned into darkness, and the moon into blood, before the coming of the great and awesome day of the Lord. (Joel 2:28-31)

This prophecy has not yet been totally fulfilled. The good news is that you can step into this flow of Holy Spirit power and fire right now. We are living in an unprecedented time of the release of gifts, signs and wonders. Think about it. You have witnessed the sun turning to darkness and the moon to blood. In my lifetime there have been three Tetrads of Blood Moons on the appointed times of the Lord. You have to look back many centuries to see this many signs in previous times. These are signs to let us know that we can receive these gifts of dreams, visions and prophecy. We can move in the fullness of this anointing now and expect more tomorrow.

Now is the time. Now is the acceptable time Paul spoke of in 2 Corinthians 6:1-2, "*We then, as workers together with Him also plead with you not to receive the grace of God in vain. For He says: 'In an acceptable time I have heard you, and in the day of salvation I have helped you.' Behold, now is the accepted time; behold, now is the day of salvation.*" We are not looking in hope for a day to come at some distant time in the future. We are standing by faith knowing that this is the "accepted time" to receive and move in all these spiritual gifts. This is the day of salvation for the lost on earth. We are called and empowered to accomplish it. Amen?

AN EVER INCREASING FIRE:

Now, Lord, consider their threats and enable your servants to speak your word with great boldness. Stretch out your hand to heal and perform miraculous signs and wonders through the name of your holy servant Jesus." *After they prayed, the place where they were meeting was shaken. And they were all filled with the Holy Spirit and spoke the word of God boldly.* (Acts 4:29-31, NIV)

The passage above is an account of the second outpouring of the Holy Spirit which came to the disciples. They continued to receive more and more. They prayed to have boldness to proclaim the name of Yeshua during a season of great persecution. We are also living in a time of great persecution. If you are willing to be bold in your proclamations of the kingdom of God, He is willing to bless you with more power, more grace, and more fire.

Remember the promise released in James 4:6, "*But He gives more grace. Therefore He says: 'God resists the proud, but gives grace to the humble.'*" In humility, we can approach the Lord, and then ask and expect to receive the same results as they experienced. We should be expecting more and more fire! Believe and receive this prayer from Psalm 115:14-15, "*May the Lord give you increase more and more, you and your children. May you be blessed by the Lord, Who made heaven and earth.*" Do you believe this? Then receive it right now and expect it over and over in the future. Amen?

AN ALL POWERFUL BLAZING FIRE

After this I looked, and there before me was a door standing open in heaven. And the voice I had first heard speaking to me like a trumpet said, "Come up here, and I will show you what must take place after this." At once I was in the Spirit, and there before me was a throne in heaven with someone sitting on it. And the one who sat there had the appearance of jasper and carnelian. A rainbow, resembling an emerald, encircled the throne. Surrounding the throne were twenty-four other thrones, and seated on them were twenty-four elders. They were dressed in white and had crowns of gold on their heads. From the throne came flashes of lightning, rumblings and peals of thunder. Before the throne, seven lamps were blazing. These are the seven spirits of God. (Revelation 4:1-5, NIV)

Have you seen the door open in heaven? If not, speak to your spiritual eyes and command them to open up and see it. Remember that God tore the Heavens open when Yeshua was baptized (Mark 1:10, NIV, *"As Jesus was coming up out of the water, he saw heaven being torn open and the Spirit descending on him like a dove."*) Search the Scriptures and you will find that this opening has not been closed. It is still there for you.

I pray that you will look up and see it. I pray that you will see the Lord standing in the opening. I pray that you will hear Him saying to you: "Come up here!" When John experienced this, he saw something very special. He saw the Holy Spirit standing before the Lord in the full mani-festation of the Seven Spirits of God. These seven spirits were not just gently burning like the last light of a natural candle. They were "blazing" before the Lord. Their power was being revealed in the fire which John saw. This is the power and the fire the Lord wants to release to you. In fact, He has already done it. These Seven Spirits have been sent out by the Lord into all the earth. Receive them and the fire right now. Amen?

A FIRE WHICH OPENS HEAVEN
VISION REPORT
WHITE ROSE

The week before we departed for a revival in Florida, I had a very powerful vision that I didn't understand. I saw a white rosebud on a long stem seemingly floating in the heavens. As I watched, it began to open up and I saw a very beautiful white rose. When it was fully opened, a white flame emerged and I saw above it an opening into heaven. I struggled trying to go through the opening but could not. It was like a swirling tunnel through dark clouds opening into a beautiful and warmly lit place of wonderful brightness. The swirling opening was filled with orange and yellow hues varying in color through the various levels of this portal into heaven.

A brightness from heaven came down on me. I had no idea what this vision meant. During our time in the revival, one of the speakers told of a similar vision with a red rose. He didn't understand it, so he asked God what it meant and received a word about revival fires. I felt foolish for not asking God the meaning of my vision. That night I asked God to reveal the meaning of the vision of the white rose to me. I saw it all again very clearly, and was told that the white rose was the budding of a pure church. When it is fully opened in purity, the Shekinah glory will emerge from it and open heaven for the light of God to pour down on the ministry of His church.

Are you ready to open up in purity like that rose? Each one of us is part of the whole body of Christ. If the church is going to open up to this anointing, we must each do the same thing. Are you ready to walk in purity? Are you ready to walk on the highway of Holiness? Are you ready to be set on fire for the Lord? Remember that this is the acceptable time. This is the day of salvation. We are living in the last days, and we need to move in great power, great grace, and great fire! Amen?

(End of Vision Report)
PRAYER

Lord, help us to be ready. Send a fresh anointing of the Holy Spirit. Send a fresh outpouring of fire. Let your fire burn away all the chaff in our hearts and minds. Let any lack of faith be consumed in the fire. Let all bitterness, jealousy, strife, envy, and unforgiveness be set ablaze and be totally removed. Please give us a fresh anointing on a regular basis so that we will be strong enough in faith to proclaim your Name in boldness regardless of the persecution which may follow. Lord, open our eyes to see, our ears to hear, and our hearts to perceive all the miracles, signs, and wonders you are releasing in our time. Help us to fully understand that this is the acceptable time and we are those called to do your work in this generation. Hear us as we cry out for more. We ask all these things in the mighty name of Yeshua ha Messiach. We believe it. We receive it, and we give you thanks for it even before it manifests. Amen and Amen!

PAUSE AND REFLECT

1. Describe one of your experiences with the fire of God.

2. Name some of the benefits from the fire of God.

3. How does the fire purify you?

4. How has the fire of the Lord set you free?

5. Describe a time when you received more fire?

6. Have you been praying for more and accepting it by faith?

CHAPTER SEVEN

THE ONE WHO BRINGS FIRE

VISION REPORT
A CALL TO PRAY

Today, the Lord made a much stronger call on my heart to pray for the nations of Israel and South Korea. As I prayed, the Lord put it into my heart to use the words of prophecy concerning Yeshua ha Messiach found in Isaiah 11:2. I was instructed to pray this for both Israel and South Korea: "*The Spirit of the Lord shall rest upon Him, The Spirit of wisdom and understanding, The Spirit of counsel and might, The Spirit of knowledge and of the fear of the Lord.*" Afterward I prayed it over the USA. I am praying this right now. Will you join me in this prayer? Begin by praying with me for Israel and South Korea and then pray it over your nation. Every nation on earth should be under the leadership, care and provision of Yeshua ha Messiach and their leaders need to operate with the same spiritual gifts which were and are working through Him.

In my intercessory warfare over these nations, I prayed for God to let the Spirit of the Lord rest powerfully upon them. I prayed for the Holy Spirit to be released upon the nations along with all the spiritual manifestations revealed through Isaiah the prophet. There is a great need today in all nations for wisdom, understanding, counsel, might, knowledge, and the fear of the Lord. The Lord had previously revealed to me that the nations of Israel and South Korea are keys to the beginning of the great end-time harvest. The Lord's timing calls for this to begin now. I felt the urgency of knowing that it is at hand, and our need to be prepared to move with it.

After praying this prayer, I was caught up by the Holy Spirit into the third heaven. I found myself bowing before the throne of Jesus. It was an awesome and majestic scene in Heaven this morning. The throne was beautiful and amazingly high. Then I saw Jesus high and lifted up over the throne. I fell before Him and worshipped with all my heart as I gave thanksgiving and praise to Him. I was expecting Him to say something that would relate to the message for today, but that didn't happen. As I watched, He silently looked over His kingdom and His people as if making a final assessment of the readiness of His church. Are you ready for His next move of the Spirit?

There was a great peace about Him. I was very pleasantly surprised to see that He had a look of profound satisfaction on His face. It filled me with joy to see Him like this. It was awesome to think that He is satisfied with the work you and I are doing and the witness we are sharing. This was somewhat surprising considering some of the things going on in His church today. Somehow, He sees us more for what we can be in the Spirit than what we currently are in the natural. I pray that we will be able to rise up to the level of His expectation. Will you pray this with me?

Then the message I received yesterday came back to my mind and my spirit. In that time with the Lord, He had taught me the importance of just being focused on spending time with Him. This morning, I knew that all I wanted was Him. I desired more than anything to just be in His presence. I am seeking His face. What more could I desire that this? So, I just spent time worshipping Him. As I gave honor, glory, majesty and praise to Him, a great sense of His shalom came over me. I was so content to be in His presence. At that moment, I knew that this is the ultimate desire of the reborn spirit – to just be with Him.

As I was allowed to continue in His presence, He stretched out His arms with His palms facing upward and lovingly said, "Come to me!" Others began to join me before the Lord. I was aware that you were there as well. After a time, He again reached out to others saying, "Come to me!" His voice was so loving and carried the powerful message of His desire to have His bride with him. More came and we worshipped together before the Lord. Can you hear it? The body of Christ is being called to draw near to the Bridegroom.

Then a third time He stretched forth His hands making a stronger plea, and saying, *"Come to Me, all you who labor and are heavy laden, and I will give you rest. Take My yoke upon you and learn from Me, for I am gentle and lowly in heart, and you will find rest for your souls. For My yoke is easy and My burden is light."* (Matthew 11:28-30) More came and worshipped the Lord. Each time more came, the Lord's joy increased. I realized at a much deeper level how important it is to Him for us to spend time in His presence.

I noticed that when His joy increased, my joy increased as well. Then I became aware that in His presence – in the intimacy of our worship before Him – we truly begin to feel what He feels – to love what He loves – and to care intensely for what He desires. It is such an awesome thought. I know this is what it means to have the heart of Jesus. This is what Paul was talking about when he said,

"But we all, with unveiled face, beholding as in a mirror the glory of the Lord, are being transformed into the same image from glory to glory, just as by the Spirit of the Lord." (2 Corinthians 3:18) As we are in Him, and He in us, we truly begin to see His glory reflected in our own image.

May you go *"from glory to glory just as by the Spirit of the Lord!"* May you experience being in His presence today! May you experience being fully in union with Him as you worship in the beauty of Holiness! May the very image of the glory of Christ be reflected in you today! May it be so strong that everyone you meet will be drawn to His presence and enter into His worship! Amen!

(End of Vision Report)
BEING "IN EXPECTATION"

> *Now as the people were **in expectation**, and all reasoned in their hearts about John, whether he was the Christ or not, John answered, saying to all, "I indeed baptize you with water; but One mightier than I is coming, whose sandal strap I am not worthy to loose. He will baptize you with the Holy Spirit and fire. His winnowing fan is in His hand, and He will thoroughly clean out His threshing floor, and gather the wheat into His barn; but the chaff He will burn with unquenchable fire."*
> (Luke 3:15-17)

I like the way the passage above begins. The phrase, "as the people were in expectation," releases to us an important Kingdom Key. Expectation opens the door for revelation. Expectation leads people to ask some important questions. As they get focused on their circumstances and the possibilities presented by the prophet, their hearts are prepared to hear from Heaven. Many were probably disappointed that John was not the promised Messiah. His bold declarations, his condemnation of the sins of the nation and its leaders, and his unusual personal appearance all spoke of something new which was about to manifest.

I didn't grow up this way. People in the church didn't seem to be expecting much of anything except just doing business as usual. The religious spirit had lulled most of us to sleep. We weren't really watching and waiting for the next coming of Messiah. We were very content with the way things were. In that environment, I grew up with a childish and very limited picture of who Jesus is. I was taught that He was a little child who grew up to be meek and mild. Now I know that this is not a very honest Biblical picture of the coming Warrior King, Yeshua ha Messiach. As far as I could determine, we were not expecting any of our chaff to be burned in an unquenchable fire. What are you expecting in this hour?

After being baptized with the Holy Spirit and with fire, my mind and spirit were opened to a very different picture of Jesus. What I had been taught didn't really account for some of the things Jesus did. How could this meek and mild Jesus make a whip, overturn tables, and drive vendors from the Temple? How could this meek and weak Jesus stand up to and out maneuver the leading scribes, Pharisees, Sadducees, Herodians, and lawyers of His day? There didn't seem to be much of an explanation available about this very different image of Jesus. As I began to study the Bible intensely, I came to understand how limited my view had been.

In the Revelation of John, we are introduced to Jesus, the powerful leader of the Church of the First Born. He is revealed as a warrior King who will see every other king and leader on earth bow before Him and declare that He is King of kings and Lord of lords. In the Revelation, I see a conquering king who will personally tread the great winepress of the wrath of God. He will stand before all the armies of the Antichrist and defeat them instantly with the powerful sword which comes from His mouth. The hosts of Heaven and the saints will accompany Him as witnesses, but He doesn't need their help to win the greatest battle of the ages. He conquered sin, death, hell and the grave for you and for me and He is returning soon to take us to our new home with Him. Amen?

> *Therefore God also has highly exalted Him and given Him the name which is above every name, that at the name of Jesus every knee should bow, of those in heaven, and of those on earth, and of those under the earth, and that every tongue should confess that Jesus Christ is Lord, to the glory of God the Father.* (Philippians 2:9-11)

God the Father has exalted Yeshua above every other person who has ever lived. He has given Him a name above every other name in heaven and on the earth. A day is coming when we will see all knees bowed before Him. A time is near when every tongue will proclaim that Yeshua is Adonai. This will not only happen on the earth but also in the underworld. There will be no exceptions. This is who Jesus is. He is all this and so much more. He is too great for us to comprehend now, but one day we will all know Him for who He is, what He has done, what He is doing and what He will do in the future. I know one thing. I want to be with Him when He returns. How about you?

Even now Yeshua is the head of the church, but many people act as if they are in charge. People talk with terms like: my church; my ministry; my gifts, however it is not about you or me. Compared to Him we have nothing. It is all about Him, and I want you to know and understand that He is not happy with much that is going around in the name of religion. Through John, He released a powerful revelation, and many in the body of Christ have not even bothered to study it. He sent letters to the seven churches which I believe represent the church in this age. Each of these churches has some good, but also need some improvement. We are wise to study what He says to the churches and let a little of the fire in His voice speak to our hearts and rekindle the flame of God in us. It is time for His disciples to be ablaze with the power and presence of the Holy Spirit and fire.

TO THE CHURCH AT EPHESUS

I know your works, your labor, your patience, and that you cannot bear those who are evil. And you have tested those who say they are apostles and are not, and have found them liars; and you have persevered and have patience, and have labored for My name's sake and have not become weary. (Revelation 2:2-3)

The church at Ephesus was not all bad. They had some good qualities. Many people today are fairly content with that. They believe it is okay to have a little bad as long as there is some good mixed with it. We could look at what Jesus said in the passage above and believe that we are doing pretty well overall. Many people believe that if they have done these good things they will surely get a passing grade on the Day of Judgment. Right? Not really.

This idea doesn't actually work with Jesus. We are not called to tolerate and ignore the shortcomings in our lives and especially not in the body of Christ. We need to hear the Lords "nevertheless" and what follows it. He will make it clear how far many of the people in His church have fallen. It will not be pleasant to hear this from the Lord before His judgment seat. In these last days, we cannot afford to lose our "first love." If you lose that love, there is nothing to replace it now or in all eternity. It is time to rekindle the fires of our relationship with Him. Think about all of these things as you read the words of Jesus to the church. What can a church possibly do if it loses its lampstand (the presence and fire of the Holy Spirit)?

> *Nevertheless I have this against you, that you have left your first love. Remember therefore from where you have fallen; repent and do the first works, or else I will come to you quickly and remove your lampstand from its place—unless you repent. But this you have, that you hate the deeds of the Nicolaitans, which I also hate.* (Revelation 2:4-5)

TO THE CHURCH AT PERGAMOS

> *I know your works, and where you dwell, where Satan's throne is. And you hold fast to My name, and did not deny My faith even in the days in which Antipas was My faithful martyr, who was killed among you, where Satan dwells.* (Revelation 2:13)

Once again we see that pesky mixture of good and bad things. As we look at it, the good seems so very good. Surely this is okay with the Lord? Even when one of their members was martyred, they did not deny their faith in the Lord Jesus. During His earthly ministry, Jesus warned about the leaven of false teaching based on manmade doctrines. Consider what He said in Matthew 16:6, "*Then Jesus said to them, 'Take heed and beware of the leaven of the Pharisees and the Sadducees.'*" Paul expanded on this teaching in Galatians 5:9, "*A little leaven leavens the whole lump.*" A little false teaching and acceptance of sin will make the whole group sinful and disobedient. This is exactly what was happening in the church at Pergamos.

> *But I have a few things against you, because you have there those who hold the doctrine of Balaam, who taught Balak to put a stumbling block before the children of Israel, to eat things sacrificed to idols, and to commit sexual immorality. Thus you also have those who hold the doctrine of the Nicolaitans, which thing I hate. Repent, or else I will come to you quickly and will fight against them with the sword of My mouth.* (Revelation 2:14-16)

The doctrine of Balaam is false teaching which comes directly against the Spirit of truth. Balaam had been offered a great reward to bring a curse on Israel, but the Lord would not let Him curse those He had blessed. Balaam persisted because he wanted the reward. He made a plan to tempt the men of Israel into sexual immorality in order to bring a curse upon themselves. The Lord will not tolerate immoral teachings even if you have done other good things. Remember the message in Jude 1:11, "*Woe to them! For they have gone in the way of Cain, have run greedily in the error of Balaam for profit, and perished in the rebellion of Korah."* The church must stay free from greed, false teaching and sexual immorality to be pleasing to the Lord.

TO THE CHURCH AT THYATIRA

> *And to the angel of the church in Thyatira write, These things says the Son of God, who has eyes like a flame of fire, and His feet like fine brass: "I know your works, love, service, faith, and your patience; and as for your works, the last are more than the first."* (Revelation 2:18-19)

As you look carefully at the list of positive things the Lord said about this church, it seems like they are doing very well. They have works, love, service, faith and patience. Not only that but they seem to be getting better with time. Yet, they are not pleasing to the Lord. Works alone will not make an individual or a church righteous. Faith and service alone will not make you completely right with the Lord. Even love and patience are inadequate when evil is tolerated in the church. Many churches struggle with this. They don't want to lose key people. The problem is that some of the people who support the church financially are operating with a controlling spirit. The Jezebel spirit is a spirit of control. If left unchecked, it will push the church away from the truth of the gospel.

> *Nevertheless I have a few things against you, because you allow that woman Jezebel,*

who calls herself a prophetess, to teach and seduce My servants to commit sexual immorality and eat things sacrificed to idols. And I gave her time to repent of her sexual immorality, and she did not repent. Indeed I will cast her into a sickbed, and those who commit adultery with her into great tribulation, unless they repent of their deeds. I will kill her children with death, and all the churches shall know that I am He who searches the minds and hearts. And I will give to each one of you according to your works. (Revelation 2:20-23)

The consequences for allowing wickedness in the body of Christ are severe. Sickness and death characterize this kind of church. Sometimes we see a church which seems to be doing all the right things, but none of the spiritual gifts seem to be working in their group. Few if any healings are ever seen. Even though they support missions, they have no impact on the nations. You cannot hide secret sins from the Lord. He sees right through all your efforts to cover them over with lies. Many churches will have to go through some serious soul searching and repentance if they want to fulfill their mission for the Kingdom of God.

TO THE CHURCH AT SARDIS

And to the angel of the church in Sardis write, these things says He who has the seven Spirits of God and the seven stars: I know your works, that you have a name that you are alive, but you are dead. Be watchful, and strengthen the things which remain, that are ready to die, for I have not found your works perfect before God. Remember therefore how you have received and heard; hold fast and repent. Therefore if you will not watch, I will come upon you as a thief, and you will not know what hour I will come upon you. (Revelation 3:1-3)

Did you notice a switch in how the Lord deals with this church? He gives the bad news first and then shares a few good things. It seems that things are worse in this church than in the others. They needed a powerful wakeup call and the Lord gave it to them. It would be painful for any church to hear this report from the Lord. Most of us have seen some churches like this which have a great reputation in the world, but have compromised in order to look good. Inside they are filled with terrible deeds. In this church there are only a few people who are obedient to the Lord. There is hope for these few faithful followers, but not much for the rest of the group unless they repent quickly. Only those who overcome the evil things of the flesh will be clothed with "white garments" which signify holiness.

You have a few names even in Sardis who have not defiled their garments; and they shall walk with Me in white, for they are worthy. He who overcomes shall be clothed in white garments, and I will not blot out his name from the Book of Life; but I will confess his name before My Father and before His angels. (Revelation 3:4-5)

TO THE CHURCH AT PHILADELPHIA

And to the angel of the church in Philadelphia write, These things says He who is holy, He who is true, He who has the key of David, He who opens and no one shuts, and shuts and no one opens: I know your works. See, I have set before you an open door, and no one can shut it; for you have a little strength, have kept My word, and have not denied My name. Indeed I will make those of the synagogue of Satan, who say they are Jews and are not, but lie—indeed I will make them come and worship before your feet, and to know that I have loved you. (Revelation 3:7-9)

The message of the Lord to this church is very different. There are no judgments for them. The only caution is for them to persevere to the end. It is possible to please the Lord and to live in a way which honors Him and Father God. These are the ones who were pleasing to the Lord in the vision at the beginning of this chapter. A day is coming when those who have stood against a church like this will come and bow at their feet, and they will finally know how much the Lord loves you. A promise like this can keep you going for a long time. It is good to be faithful to the Lord because He will always give you more than He asks of you. Look at the other blessings coming to the church at Philadelphia.

Because you have kept My command to persevere, I also will keep you from the hour of trial which shall come upon the whole world, to test those who dwell on the earth. Behold,

I am coming quickly! Hold fast what you have, that no one may take your crown. He who overcomes, I will make him a pillar in the temple of My God, and he shall go out no more. I will write on him the name of My God and the name of the city of My God, the New Jerusalem, which comes down out of heaven from My God. And I will write on him My new name. (Revelation 3:10-12)

TO THE CHURCH AT LAODICEA

Perhaps the harshest judgment falls on the seventh church in this list. Some people think they can play it safe by not doing anything too bad – a little good mixed with a little bad. They play it safe by not doing enough to be criticized by the world. They want to keep life easy and have a smooth relationship with the world and the flesh. The message to this church reminds us that a lifestyle of appeasement will not be blessed by the Lord. Lukewarm churches are so offensive to the Lord that He wants to vomit them out. This is crude imagery but very descriptive of the Lord's feelings about those who have become lukewarm. It calls us to think carefully about how we are serving the Lord.

I know your works, that you are neither cold nor hot. I could wish you were cold or hot. So then, because you are lukewarm, and neither cold nor hot, I will vomit you out of My mouth. Because you say, 'I am rich, have become wealthy, and have need of nothing'—and do not know that you are wretched, miserable, poor, blind, and naked—I counsel you to buy from Me gold refined in the fire, that you may be rich; and white garments, that you may be clothed, that the shame of your nakedness may not be revealed; and anoint your eyes with eye salve, that you may see. (Revelation 3:15-18)

SUMMARY FOR THE CHURCHES

As many as I love, I rebuke and chasten. Therefore be zealous and repent. Behold, I stand at the door and knock. If anyone hears My voice and opens the door, I will come in to him and dine with him, and he with Me. To him who overcomes I will grant to sit with Me on My throne, as I also overcame and sat down with My Father on His throne. "He who has an ear, let him hear what the Spirit says to the churches. (Revelation 3:19-22)

Many times Yeshua made the same statement we see in Revelation 3:22, *"He who has an ear, let him hear ..."* Sometimes we may wonder if anyone is really listening to our sermons and teachings. The behavior of some people may cause you to wonder if they really have ears to hear. Instead of looking at the speck in our neighbor's eye, Jesus is calling us to get the log out of our own eye as a first step. It is important for us to hear this: *As many as I love, I rebuke and chasten."* We should not run away from the Lord's rebuke. It comes from His love and His desire for us to succeed in our destiny for the Kingdom.

Just as all the behaviors which look good are not necessarily good, a rebuke or chastening is not necessarily a bad thing. The Lord chastens those He loves. Think about that as you study these things. Read the passage below from the Book of Hebrews and combine the message with the one from Yeshua in the Revelation. We must always remain open to his guidance and discipline if we want to be all He has called us to be.

> *And you have forgotten that word of encouragement that addresses you as sons: "My son, do not make light of the Lord's discipline, and do not lose heart when he rebukes you, because the Lord disciplines those he loves, and he punishes everyone he accepts as a son."* (Hebrews 12:5-6)

END-TIME PICTURE OF JESUS

In the Revelation of John, we're introduced to the end-time picture of Jesus as the conquering King of kings and Lord of Lords. Study the two passages below and think about how Jesus is presented by John. Meek and mild does not even come close to adequately describing the great conquering King who is returning to rule and reign on earth. He will come with power and great glory. He will return as the commander of the Hosts of Heaven. He will return as the judge and the advocate for all His followers. He will have all authority in Heaven and on earth. All knees will bow to Him. Amen?

> *I saw heaven standing open and there before me was a white horse, whose rider is called Faithful and True. With justice he judges and wages war. His eyes are like blazing fire, and on his head are many crowns. He has a name written on him that no one knows but*

he himself. He is dressed in a robe dipped in blood, and his name is the Word of God. The armies of heaven were following him, riding on white horses and dressed in fine linen, white and clean. (Revelation 19:11-14, NIV)

Now out of His mouth goes a sharp sword, that with it He should strike the nations. And He Himself will rule them with a rod of iron. He Himself treads the winepress of the fierceness and wrath of Almighty God. And He has on His robe and on His thigh a name written: KING OF KINGS AND LORD OF LORDS. (Revelation 19:15-16)

Are these passages meant to be scary images of Jesus? No! They are to give you assurance and to build your faith. Declare and decree with me: My God is a mighty God who wins the victory for me! Hallelujah! This is the purpose for these images. They are to be frightening for those who are living as His enemies. He will be more frightening than these images when disobedient and rebellious people see Him face to face. But to His followers, He will still be the Good Shepard who always cares for His precious sheep.

As some people read these descriptions of Jesus they think that perhaps He has changed. What do you think? Did Jesus change? No!!! We have a promise. Read it aloud over and over from Hebrews 13:8, *"Jesus Christ is the same yesterday, today, and forever."* The problem is not with Jesus. The problem is with people who try to make him more politically correct, more inclusive, and more tolerant than He is or will be. They want a king who is like a benign and forgetful old man who will tolerate their misdeeds if they learn to appease Him. Nothing could be further from the truth.

Many people want a God who is extremely tolerant and nonthreatening! They have worked hard to design and sell a picture which makes Him appear to be weak and powerless! Here is the problem. That's not my Jesus! You cannot change Him. You need to be asking Him to change you. Look at what He says about Himself. "*I have come to bring fire on the earth, and how I wish it were already kindled!*" (Luke 12:49) Jesus is the primary fire starter! Are you ready to be a fire starter?

Jesus had to wait to get the fire started! It all had to be in Father God's timing and in accordance with His plan. In Luke 12:50, Jesus said, "*But I have a baptism to be baptized with, and how distressed I am till it is accomplished!*" Of course, He was speaking of His death on the cross and His resurrection from the dead. Those events are now in the past. Now He is kindling that fire He spoke of from the beginning. Are you ready for it? Are you ready to be set on fire for the Lord?

I have some bad news for the appeasers, the man pleasers, and the political correctness police. Jesus is a source of division! "*Do you think I came to bring peace on earth? No, I tell you, but division.*" (Luke 12:51, NIV) Think about it. Jesus was not mincing words. He was making it very plain that the things of God are not designed with the ultimate purpose of appeasing the sensibilities of modern man. He is never going to change the gospel of the kingdom of God to fit into the culture of the flesh. He is calling the culture to mold itself into the image of the Kingdom. In the two following verses, Jesus described how divisive the gospel of the Kingdom may be in some families.

For from now on five in one house will be divided: three against two, and two against three. Father will be divided against son and son against father, mother against daughter and daughter against mother, mother-in-law against her daughter-in-law and daughter-in-law against her mother-in-law. (Luke 12:52-53)

The Lord is not bringing division for the sake of division. He is simply making it clear that the cultures and philosophies of this world have strayed from the truth. He will not change the truth to make people happy. He is calling people to open their eyes and ears to see and hear the truth. He is calling people to open their spirits and minds to the ultimate truths of eternity. Not everyone will be offended, and there is a blessing for those who do not take offense. Remember what Jesus said in Matthew 11:6, *"And blessed is he who is not offended because of Me."*

John answered them all, "I baptize you with water. But one who is more powerful than I will come, the straps of whose sandals I am not worthy to untie. He will baptize you with the Holy Spirit and fire. His winnowing fork is in his hand to clear his threshing floor and to gather the wheat into his barn, but he will burn up the chaff with unquenchable fire." (Luke 3:16-17, NIV)

Are you ready for the fire of God? When I was young, I really liked the children's game "Hide and Seek." Remember that famous challenge: "Ready or not, here I come!" I am hearing the Lord speak these words now.

I pray that we will be ready. I am pressing in to it and asking for more of the fire of God. How about you? I am also praying for you to receive more fire. I will conclude this chapter by asking once again: Are you ready to step into Holy Spirit fire?

PRAYER

He who testifies to these things says, "Surely I am coming quickly." Amen. Even so, come, Lord Jesus! The grace of our Lord Jesus Christ be with you all. Amen. (Revelation 22:20-21)

Father God I ask you right now to help us to become ready for the return of our Lord, Jesus. Help us by baptizing us afresh with the Holy Spirit and with fire. Please burn away everything which is not of you. Burn away everything which hinders our walk with you. Lord we are asking for supernatural boldness to proclaim the name of Yeshua ha Messiach. We are asking for our preaching and teaching of the gospel of the Kingdom to be accompanied by healings, miracles, signs and wonders which will confirm the message in the hearts of unbelievers. Lord we want to serve in the great end-time harvest to win souls for the Kingdom. Please shape us, equip us, train us, and prepare us to be effective ministers of the gospel of Yeshua ha Messiach. It is in his holy name we pray! Amen and Amen!

PAUSE AND REFLECT

1. Summarize Jesus' message to the church at Ephesus!

2. Summarize Jesus' message to the church at Pergamos!

3. Summarize Jesus' message to the church at Laodicea!?

4. In your own words give a description of Jesus in the last days?

5. Why is the gospel so divisive?

6. How are you preparing your heart to receive the fire of the Holy Spirit?

7. Are you ready to step into Holy Spirit fire?

CHAPTER EIGHT

WHAT DELAYS REVIVAL

Then one was brought to Him who was demon-possessed, blind and mute; and He healed him, so that the blind and mute man both spoke and saw. And all the multitudes were amazed and said, "Could this be the Son of David?" Now when the Pharisees heard it they said, "This fellow does not cast out demons except by Beelzebub, the ruler of the demons." (Matthew 12:22-24)

The church has been crying out for many years for revival. In the last few years, it seems like the cries are getting louder and more people are pressing in for it. Groups are gathering to pray in agreement. People are decreeing it by faith. It seems like the Biblical requirements for answered prayer have all been met. Remember what Jesus taught in Matthew 18:19-20, *"Again I say to you that if two of you agree on earth concerning anything that they ask, it will be done for them by My Father in heaven. For where two or three are gathered together in My name, I am there in the midst of them."*

It seems like we are doing all the right things, but where is the revival? It seems like we have been doing these things for several years now, and we wonder when it will manifest. We have also received many prophetic words about revival coming soon. Beginning in 2010 the Lord was giving me visions of revival breaking out around the world. In the Month of August, I received eight different messages from the Lord about what should have broken out then. One of those visions was reported at the beginning of Chapter One. It would be a good idea to read it again before moving to the next section.

REVIVAL DELAY

When I received these visions, I firmly believed this outbreak of revival around the world was imminent. I was living in expectation every day for it to manifest. I continued to pray for it and press in for more from the Lord. Have you ever experienced something like this? You receive a word from the Lord and expect it to manifest long before you actually see it. This was what I was experiencing all this time. I was waiting and watching every day, but something happened to change it. So, I began to ask and seek wisdom to understand what is holding up a breakout of revival? What is restraining the fire of the Holy Spirit in this season? I'm sure there are many reasons, but one became clear in 2010. We saw strife breaking out in many churches and ministries and this blocked their season of revival.

These six things the Lord hates, yes, seven are an abomination to Him: A proud look, a lying tongue, hands that shed innocent blood, a heart that devises wicked plans, feet that are swift in running to evil, a false witness who speaks lies, and one who sows discord among brethren. (Proverbs 6:16-19)

Think about it. The enemy has somehow gotten into our camp and deceived people to enter into rebellion and strife. It occurred to me that it is something like Balaam's deception. He couldn't curse Israel because the Lord had blessed them. So, he came up with a plan to get them to block their own relationship with the Lord. This opened them up to be under the curse again. It seems like this is happening again in our time. This should not surprise us. God is creative and does new things all the time, but the enemy does the same things over and over. We need to learn from the past and stand firm with the Lord so that He can use us to begin another mighty move of the Holy Spirit and Fire.

As I reflected on the state of the body of Christ in 2010, I wondered: How could they let this happen? The real question is: How can we let it keep happening? Like a sports team which loses unexpectedly, we need to go back to the basics. Coaches don't teach trick plays or spectacular plans after a big loss. They go back to the basic principles of the sport and train their players again. This happens with professional teams. We need to learn from these powerful principles. I went back to the Word of God to see if Jesus taught about it. I found that Jesus gave a four part answer to this in the Gospel of Matthew.

JESUS' FOUR PART ANSWER
1. DIVIDED HOUSES AND KINGDOMS

Divided houses and divided kingdoms cannot stand. They are in the process of falling as soon as division begins to manifest. When this happens, they will most certainly fail to achieve their goals and purposes. This is true for the body of Christ as well. To make it personal: It is true for you and me.

> *But Jesus knew their thoughts, and said to them: "Every kingdom divided against itself is brought to desolation, and every city or house divided against itself will not stand. If Satan casts out Satan, he is divided against himself. How then will his kingdom stand? And if I cast out demons by Beelzebub, by whom do your sons cast them out? Therefore they shall be your judges. But if I cast out demons by the Spirit of God, surely the kingdom of God has come upon you. Or how can one enter a strong man's house and plunder his goods, unless he first binds the strong man? And then he will plunder his house. He who is not with Me is against Me, and he who does not gather with Me scatters abroad.* (Matthew 12:25-30)

We see so many families splitting up today. Some statistics say that more marriages fail than succeed. In our families and in our churches, we lament this happening to those we love. Marital breakups cause so much pain and do such great damage to everyone involved. Often the children are hurt the worst. Many of these children grow up feeling that they are somehow responsible for the family not being able to stay together. Unless these things are resolved, some of them will remain wounded throughout their lives. Many churches are developing and conducting programs to bring healing to those hurt in this manner. That is good, but we need to do more. We need to help families to become healed before the breakup. We need to get back into the restoration business. We need to go back to the basics of our faith and the basic principles taught in the Word of God.

> *Brothers (and sisters), if someone is caught in a sin, you who are spiritual should restore him gently. But watch yourself, or you also may be tempted. Carry each other's burdens, and in this way you will fulfill the law of Christ. If anyone thinks he is something when he is nothing, he deceives himself. Each one should test his own actions. Then he can take pride in himself, without comparing himself to somebody else, for each one should carry his own load. (Galatians 6:1-5, NIV)*

Many nations which were once strong and united have fallen under the same divisive spirit. One of the primary manifestations of this spiritual disorder can be seen when almost everyone is blaming and accusing others for their problems. Remember the enemy is known as "the accuser." When we begin to place blame on others, we are doing his work. He has gotten inside our once secure boundaries and is wreaking havoc on our unity and strength. Many churches and nations are in great turmoil and are hovering on the edge of collapse.

When churches and believers allow this to happen, they are quenching the Holy Spirit and His fire. These forces sometimes seem out of control and beyond our ability to bring healing. What are we to do? How can we overcome these powerful forces which are bringing so much pain and division on us? How can we get back on track with the Holy Spirit and the Fire of God to bring revival in our homes, churches, and nations? I found some great advice from Paul in the passage below.

> *Now we exhort you, brethren, warn those who are unruly, comfort the fainthearted, uphold the weak, be patient with all. See that no one renders evil for evil to anyone, but always pursue what is good both for yourselves and for all. Rejoice always, pray without ceasing, in everything give thanks; for this is the will of God in Christ Jesus for you. Do not quench the Spirit. Do not despise prophecies. Test all things; hold fast what is good. Abstain from every form of evil. (1 Thessalonians 5:14-22)*

2. BLASPHEMING THE HOLY SPIRIT

Blasphemy against the Holy Spirit will bring you back under the curse. This is so powerful and most churches are not really teaching this. The manmade doctrine of unconditional grace has robbed us of our sensitivity to the truth of the Word of God. As in these Biblical lessons, we see people today who are actually accusing Jesus of false teaching, because what He said doesn't line up with their "feel good theology." We need to cast off every manmade doctrine and get back to the truth. Remember, Jesus is the truth. Listen to what He says about blasphemy.

> *Therefore I say to you, every sin and blasphemy will be forgiven men, but the blasphemy against the Spirit will not be forgiven men. Anyone who speaks a word against the Son of Man, it will be forgiven him; but*

whoever speaks against the Holy Spirit, it will not be forgiven him, either in this age or in the age to come. (Matthew 12:31-32)

Some people choose to be ignorant about this teaching. They say that we don't really know exactly what this sin is. This too is a false teaching. This word from the Lord was given as a direct response to something which happened. Look back at Matthew 12:24, "*Now when the Pharisees heard it they said, 'This fellow does not cast out demons except by Beelzebub, the ruler of the demons.'*" Jesus made it very plain to the Pharisees that what they were saying was a sin which would not be forgiven. Some people today are teaching that this cannot happen. Such teaching is manmade if it does not line up with the teachings of Jesus. Always go back to the basics of what the Lord released in His Word.

Think about it. Anytime you judge a move of God and declare that it is a move of the enemy, you have committed this sin. This will never be forgiven. It is an eternal sin. I have experienced people doing this many times. They don't fully understand the anointing or ministry of another individual and begin to accuse them of demonic things. I suppose that is possible, but this is a very dangerous thing to do. If you mislabel the work of the Holy Spirit you will quench His fire in your heart. I remind you once more of what Paul said in 1 Thessalonians 5:19-22, "*Do not quench the Spirit. Do not despise prophecies. Test all things; hold fast what is good. Abstain from every form of evil.*"

3. BEARING BAD FRUIT

Either make the tree good and its fruit good, or else make the tree bad and its fruit bad; for a tree is known by its fruit. Brood of vipers! How can you, being evil, speak good things? For out of the abundance of the heart the mouth speaks. A good man out of the good treasure of his heart brings forth good things, and an evil man out of the evil treasure brings forth evil things. (Matthew 12:33-35)

Jesus declared that we will know a tree by its fruit. There are good trees and there are bad trees. This is an unpopular teaching today. We want to believe that everyone is the same and equally good, however, this does not line up with the teachings of Jesus or with the reality of human behavior. We must choose whether it is better to be politically correct by human standards are Biblically correct by the Lord's standards. Tragically, many people today are making the wrong choice. The truth is that most of the fruit of the politically correct tree is bad fruit. It sounds good, but it isn't true. We can choose to live under an illusion and believe a lie, or we can choose the truth. Each generation faces this choice and tragically many in our generation are making poor decisions.

But He answered and said, "Every plant which My heavenly Father has not planted will be uprooted. Let them alone. They are blind leaders of the blind. And if the blind leads the blind, both will fall into a ditch." (Matthew 15:13-14)

The teaching above is also unpopular today. Many people believe they can save everyone. The truth is that you and I can save no one. Only the Lord can save, and only the Lord can decree what is good. Many people don't like to be told to give up on another person, and we must never take this lightly. It is easy to make this choice out of our own spirits and out of our own hurt feelings. This is never the correct answer. Yet, when the Lord says to leave them alone, I leave them alone. How about you?

Blind leaders cannot see the truth. Neither can they hear the truth. Until they are healed, they will remain in error. Tragically they are leading others into error. The end result is that both "fall into the ditch." So, what can we do? We need to examine ourselves and see where we are in error. We need to examine the fruit we are producing and determine the health of our own souls. We need to be ready to repent and be restored. We need to call upon the Lord for forgiveness, healing, and a fresh anointing of the Holy Spirit and of fire.

4. WRONG WORDS

But I say to you that for every idle word men may speak, they will give account of it in the day of judgment. For by your words you will be justified, and by your words you will be condemned. (Matthew 12:36-37)

This is an important and profound truth. You will be judged by your words. There is no getting around this. This doesn't really come as a big surprise. Remember what Solomon wrote in Proverbs 18:21, "*Death and life are in the power of the tongue, and those who love it will eat its fruit.*" When the prophet Isaiah encounter the fiery presence of the Lord, he felt completely "undone." He immediately saw the difference between his human character and the awesome character of God. We can learn from His experience. It is good to read it again. "*So I said: 'Woe is me, for I am undone! Because I am a man of unclean lips, and I dwell in the midst of a people of unclean lips; for my eyes have seen the King, the Lord of hosts.'*" (Isaiah 6:5)

We live in amazing times when we are once again experiencing the powerful presence of the Lord. As this happens, we may experience something like what Isaiah experienced. We live with a dilemma. By the fire of the Holy Spirit, we are compelled to speak the Word of God and at the same time fully aware of our unworthiness to do so. How can the pure Word of God pass through our perverse lips? We are challenged by what Jesus taught about the work of the mouth.

> *When He had called the multitude to Himself, He said to them, "Hear and understand: Not what goes into the mouth defiles a man; but what comes out of the mouth, this defiles a man."* (Matthew 15:10-11)

It all goes back to the heart. This is not speaking about the muscle which pumps our blood, but about our human spirits. Whatever we have stored in our hearts will come flowing out of the mouth. It can only be controlled for a limited amount of time with a great deal of tiring focus. Eventually the truth will come out. The really unfortunate thing is that what comes out of the mouth gets stored back in the heart. When perverse things come out and then return, there is something like a double-portion anointing on these words. This is a double-portion we do not want to have in our hearts. If we continue to speak this way, matters will continue to get worse. Study the passage below and see how David sought the help of the Lord to deal with this problem.

> *Set a guard, O LORD, over my mouth; keep watch over the door of my lips. Do not incline my heart to any evil thing, to practice wicked works with men who work iniquity; and do not let me eat of their delicacies.* (Psalm 141:3-4)

The things which come out of our own mouths can defile us. This is much more of a problem than eating some kind of unclean food. We need to watch both, but we need to watch our words more. These words can do more damage than most people believe. Peter struggled to understand this teaching of Jesus and asked for help. Perhaps we need to ask for help also so that we can speak the things which please the Lord and bless others.

> *Then Peter answered and said to Him, "Explain this parable to us." So Jesus said, "Are you also still without understanding? Do you not yet understand that whatever enters the mouth goes into the stomach and is eliminated? But those things which proceed out of the mouth come from the heart, and they defile a man. For out of the heart proceed evil thoughts, murders, adulteries, fornications, thefts, false witness, blasphemies. These are the things which defile a man, but to eat with unwashed hands does not defile a man."* (Matthew 15:15-20)

We simply cannot carry the fire of revival unless we deal with this issue. Isaiah quickly saw that he could not speak the pure word of God with defiled lips. How much do you and I need to be healed in this area? Isaiah had already been speaking the Word of the Lord, however when he experienced the fire and the holiness of the Lord, he had a clear picture of his shortcomings. Like Isaiah, we need to have an experience which makes this real for us so that we become ready to receive the refining and purify fire we desperately need.

ADDITIONAL ROADBLOCKS TO REVIVAL
1. A SPIRIT OF OFFENSE

Jesus answered and said to them, "Go and tell John the things which you hear and see: The blind see and the lame walk; the lepers are cleansed and the deaf hear; the dead are raised up and the poor have the gospel preached to them. And blessed is he who is not offended because of Me." (Matthew 11:4-6)

Taking offense can block you from receiving what the Lord is trying to release to you. Taking offense can hinder you from really understanding who Yeshua is. Taking offense can keep you from receiving your miracle. It can block you from receiving your healing. This is such a powerful and destructive emotional response. It basically blocks the flow of the positive elements in a relationship. It is critically important for us to rid ourselves of this kind of response if we want to experience and host revival. Ironically, religious leaders are often the ones most prone to responding with offense.

> *Then His disciples came and said to Him, "Do You know that the Pharisees were offended when they heard this saying?"*(Matthew 15:12)

Think about it. This is the work of the religious spirit. This spirit constantly works to tempt people to compare a new move of God with a former one. It sets up a form of legalism which rejects all new things. Most of us have heard what has been described as one of the laws of the church: "We never did it that way before." This is usually said by a group resisting a new move of the Lord. This kind of response is especially tragic when you consider again what the Lord said in Revelation 21:5 "*Then He who sat on the throne said, 'Behold, I make all things new.' And He said to me, 'Write, for these words are true and faithful.'*" If you have difficulty accepting the new things of God, you are going to have a continuous struggle. He is doing new things all the time. Get over it and get on with revival! Amen?

In revival, we are often focused on soul winning. When large numbers of people get born again and added to our numbers, this is usually viewed as a sign of revival. Most believers want to win souls, but are unaware of how they may be blocking themselves from fulfilling this desire because of a spirit of offense. Consider the teaching in Proverbs 18:19, "*A brother offended is harder to win than a strong city, and contentions are like the bars of a castle.*" If you behave in a way which is offensive to an unbeliever, you will probably never win that person for Christ.

We need to avoid both giving and receiving an offense. It is important to realize that you cannot control the emotions of another person. You cannot prevent them from taking an offense. You do the best you can to lead them to the Lord while asking the Holy Spirit to complete the work. We know that a time is coming when more and more people will be offended by the gospel of the Kingdom. The Lord has warned us in advance about this season. We don't try to make it happen, but we stay aware that some things are out of our control. Don't waste time trying to deal with false guilt. Stay focused on the truth of the Gospel of the Kingdom. Be aware that offense will come, but strive to be certain it doesn't come through you.

> *And then many will be offended, will betray one another, and will hate one another. Then many false prophets will rise up and deceive many. And because lawlessness will abound, the love of many will grow cold. But he who endures to the end shall be saved.* (Matthew 24:10-13)

2. PRIDE AND ARROGANCE

> *Talk no more so very proudly; Let no arrogance come from your mouth, for the LORD is the God of knowledge; and by Him actions are weighed.* (1 Samuel 2:3)

Two of the things which will quickly block the flow of Holy Spirit fire are pride and arrogance. I list these together because they almost always come together when they manifest. The writer of Proverbs 16:18 warns of the results of these two attributes, *"Pride goes before destruction, and a haughty spirit before a fall."* The Lord will not allow people who carry these things to stand for long. They may look rock solid right now, but the fall is coming. Tragically, leaders in large revival movements can get caught up in these things. When you begin to think that a movement of revival fire cannot happen without you, your ideas, or your gifts, you have moved into dangerous territory, and a fall often follows. Remember Proverbs 8:13, "*The fear of the LORD is to hate evil; pride and arrogance and the evil way and the perverse mouth I hate.*"

Pride is a turning away from the things of the Spirit and a turning toward the things of the flesh. When the focus shifts from what the Lord is doing to what you are doing, you are walking in a dangerous place. We must never lose our awe and respect for the Lord. We must never try to take credit for what He is doing. He will not share His glory with any woman or man. There is no wisdom in pride. Proverbs 1:7, "*The fear of the Lord is the beginning of knowledge, but fools despise wisdom and instruction.*" The fear (awe) of the Lord is the beginning of wisdom and pride brings it to a close. Take to heart the teaching in 1 Peter 5:5, "*Likewise you younger people, submit your-selves to your elders. Yes, all of you be submissive to one another, and be clothed with humility, for God resists the proud, but gives grace to the humble.*"

Young revivalists often have difficulty in this area. Wisdom often comes over time with the discipline and admonition of the Lord. It takes time to shape a man or woman of God, and the patience and longsuffering of the Lord is often amazing. However, this difficulty is not limited to young people. As you get older there is a temptation to begin to focus on your own wisdom rather than continuing to see all wisdom as a gift from the Lord. When you begin to claim any of His work for yourself, pride is usually found at the root of the issue.

When children are told what to do or what not to do, they usually want to know one thing. They will ask: Why? Adults often continue to behave in childish ways, and do not want to obey until they have an answer to the "Why?" question. Normally the problem with these questions is that something else is behind them. Unbelief always lurks behind this question. As a result, no answer will satisfy the question. It takes spiritual maturity to be able to understand and accept the Lord's answer. Spiritual maturity grows as we lay aside pride and arrogance. I believe the most powerful reason for avoiding pride and arrogance is given in the passage below.

> *Thus says the Lord: "Let not the wise man glory in his wisdom, let not the mighty man glory in his might, nor let the rich man glory in his riches; but let him who glories glory in this, that he understands and knows Me, that I am the Lord, exercising lovingkindness, judgment, and righteousness in the earth. For in these I delight," says the Lord.* (Jeremiah 9:23-24)

Did you catch it? The Lord wants us to understand Him, and prideful people can't fully get his self-revelation into their minds or their spirits. The Lord wants us to know Him, but we can't really know Him when we are rejecting His Word. He has disclosed so much of Himself in the scriptures, but pride and arrogance have blocked many from receiving it. The key thing the Lord wants to reveal about Himself is that He always exercises "*lovingkindness, judgment, and righteousness in the earth.*" Doing these things for us gives Him "*delight.*" He continues to give, but pride and arrogance block many people from receiving.

3. BITTERNESS AND UNFORGIVENESS

And do not grieve the Holy Spirit of God, by whom you were sealed for the day of redemption. Let all bitterness, wrath, anger, clamor, and evil speaking be put away from you, with all malice. (Ephesians 4:30-31)

Did you notice that bitterness is the first thing on the list of attributes which grieve the Holy Spirit? Many people who don't understand this may continue to grieve the Holy Spirit without being aware of the root cause. People who are deep into bitterness are often focused on blaming others for their troubles. It is very difficult to get through their bitterness with this teaching. Even the Holy Spirit has difficulty reaching them because they have closed their spirits to His wisdom, counsel and understanding. You may have noticed the other items in this list. These often accompany the root of bitterness: *"wrath, anger, clamor, and evil speaking...with all malice."*

I believe that the grief of the Holy Spirit is threefold. First, He is grieved with the wrath and evil speaking toward the Lord's people. When you judge and condemn a brother or sister in the Lord, you are causing the Holy Spirit to feel pain. The second point of grief is the damage this does to the person who is controlled by bitterness. The Holy Spirit wants so much more of the good things of the Lord for that person, but they will not receive it. The third part of the grief is that channels of communication and instruction have been blocked and the Holy Spirit is not allowed by these individuals to get through to their spirits. It grieves the Holy Spirit when He is not allowed to provide the assistance a person needs. He has gifts to give, but they are not being received. We need to rid ourselves of all bitterness so that it will bring relief to ourselves, others and the Holy Spirit. Amen?

> *Pursue peace with all people, and holiness, without which no one will see the Lord: looking carefully lest anyone fall short of the grace of God; lest any root of bitterness springing up cause trouble, and by this many become defiled; (Hebrews 12:14-15)*

Many people like to quote verse 14 in the passage above without adding verse 15. When we pursue the Shalom of the Lord, we are set free from the things which are holding us back from true intimacy. Think about it. This is so powerful: without holiness *"no one will see the Lord."* If you continue to hold on to bitterness, it can eventually result in falling *"short of the grace of God."* Most people would agree that they do not want these things to happen, and yet many hold on to the very things which block them. Notice again the association of bitterness with this issue. Bitterness will cause trouble: for you; for others; and for the Holy Spirit. Bitterness will defile you, and block you from walking in holiness without which you cannot see the Lord. This is so important. It is imperative for everyone to get rid of bitterness and unforgiveness. Amen?

> *But know this, that in the last days perilous times will come: For men will be lovers of themselves, lovers of money, boasters, proud, blasphemers, disobedient to parents, unthankful, unholy, unloving, unforgiving, slanderers, without self-control, brutal, despisers of good, traitors, headstrong, haughty, lovers of pleasure rather*

than lovers of God, having a form of godli-
ness but denying its power. And from such
people turn away! (2 Timothy 3:1-5)

All of these things which block revival, extinguish the fire of the Lord, and prevent people from living in holiness are attributes of the enemies of God. These things will increase more and more in these last days, but we must be very careful to insure they do not come through us. You do not want to be counted among the disreputable people Paul is describing to Timothy. Having a form of godliness will never be adequate in our walk with the Lord. We are told to turn away from these people who have a form of godliness but deny its power.

4. GRUMBLING AND MURMURING

All the Israelites grumbled against Moses and
Aaron, and the whole assembly said to them,
"If only we had died in Egypt! Or in this desert!
Why is the LORD bringing us to this land only
to let us fall by the sword? Our wives and
children will be taken as plunder. Wouldn't
it be better for us to go back to Egypt?" And
they said to each other, "We should choose
a leader and go back to Egypt." (Numbers
14:2-4, NIV)

It has never been easy to lead people. From the earliest times, people being led by the Lord have been resistant to His leadership and to that of His anointed leaders. Many of those resistant to leadership are characterized in Scripture as grumblers who constantly murmur and complain about almost everything their leaders do. One of the lessons I learned in the military is that soldiers will grumble and complain, but you don't have to let it deter you from doing your duty. This is one of the challenges you must face in leadership. Imagine how much of this is directed at the Lord.

> *Then they despised the pleasant land; they did not believe his promise. They grumbled in their tents and did not obey the LORD. So he swore to them with uplifted hand that he would make them fall in the desert, make their descendants fall among the nations and scatter them throughout the lands.* (Psalm 106:24-27)

No matter how much you do for some people, they will grumble and complain. I once lead a group tasked to provide instruction to the staff in a large hospital. The members of the group wanted to make it more pleasant for the students who had to come early in the morning for the training. They started to use their own money to buy coffee and pastries for the class members. Can you guess the results? Very few of those attending ever expressed gratitude for these gifts. Most thought they deserved more items and better products and they complained continuously about not having enough of the things they liked.

The instructors thought about it and made a decision to continue to provide these gifts for the students with their own money. This too was a powerful lesson. They made a fundamental decision not to change who they were and the gifts they were providing because of the ingratitude of their students. In an even greater way, the Lord chooses not to change who He is because people are sometimes ungrateful.

But when the assembly gathered in opposition to Moses and Aaron and turned toward the Tent of Meeting, suddenly the cloud covered it and the glory of the LORD appeared. Then Moses and Aaron went to the front of the Tent of Meeting, and the LORD said to Moses, "Get away from this assembly so I can put an end to them at once." And they fell facedown. (Numbers 16:42-45, NIV)

There is a powerful lesson in the passage above. It may seem to counter what I taught in the paragraph above, but I believe it is speaking of something different. The truth is that the Lord is longsuffering, patient, kind, forgiving and merciful, but you can push Him too far. I see something more in this passage about the way the Lord was training Moses and Aaron. He put pressure on them to stand up for the people and to intercede on their behalf. They were receiving the brunt of the criticism (like my instructor staff), but they had a higher calling than to respond in anger. This is a tough lesson and few learn it very well.

*The Jews then complained about Him, because He said, "I am the bread which came down from heaven." And they said, "Is not this Jesus, the son of Joseph, whose father and mother we know? How is it then that He says, 'I have come down from heaven'?" Jesus therefore answered and said to them, "**Do not murmur** among yourselves. No one can come to Me unless the Father who sent Me draws him; and I will raise him up at the last day.* (John 6:41-44)

Jesus faced the same issues as Moses had experienced centuries early. The very people He was trying to help were murmuring, grumbling, complaining and blaming. Their own behavior and attitudes were blocking their ability to see Yeshua as the way, the truth and the life. They were missing the greatest opportunity ever given. They were seeing the Lord face to face. What an awesome gift from the Lord. They should have rejoiced, but their grumbling robbed them of the joy of this experience. They were being invited to accept Yeshua ha Messiach and receive eternal life, but they shifted to their lower nature and grumbled against Him.

There are at least two ways to look at this. You can look at their behavior and see their weaknesses and flaws. You can judge and condemn their behavior. You can focus on their failures and shortcomings, or you can try to see what this passage is saying about you. This is a good time to do some self-examination and see when you may have done the same things in your relationship with the Lord. When you see it, you can repent, ask for forgiveness, and allow the Lord to lift you up to a higher level of Glory. In so doing you may have the opportunity to learn how to respond more appropriately to His leadership. Remember what Paul taught about moving to a higher level in the glory.

But we all, with unveiled face, beholding as in a mirror the glory of the Lord, are being transformed into the same image from glory to glory, just as by the Spirit of the Lord. (2 Corinthians 3:18)

5. REBELLION

But these speak evil of whatever they do not know; and whatever they know naturally, like brute beasts, in these things they corrupt themselves. Woe to them! For they have gone in the way of Cain, have run greedily in the error of Balaam for profit, and perished in the rebellion of Korah. (Jude 1:10-11)

Rebellion is a dangerous practice. Rebellion is not for people who are weak and afraid. It is a direct attack on the Lord, His plans, and His purposes. The Lord has never been accepting of this behavior. You cannot be in rebellion and walk in holiness. It does not work that way. If you do what Korah and his followers did, you can expect the results they got. His attack on Moses and Aaron was targeted on the issue of holiness. He believed he was more holy that either of them and deserved to be in leadership. That didn't work out very well for him. He was sent directly to "the pit" while he was still alive. Everyone who had come into agreement with him took the same trip.

The Lord will not tolerate a spirit of rebellion. For a detailed study on the effects of rebellion, see my book, "A Warriors Guide to the Seven Spirits of God: Part 1, Chapter 3 "Spirit of Holiness." You can see this at work over and over throughout the Bible. From the opening passage in this section, you can see that it was still a problem in the New Testament era and it is still a problem today. The spirit of rebellion comes to deceive and lead the Lord's people into destruction. Remember what Jesus said in John 10:10a, "*The thief does not come except to steal, and to kill, and to destroy.*" The thief is real and he is still up to the same old tricks.

Then the prophet Jeremiah said to Hananiah the prophet, "Hear now, Hananiah, the LORD has not sent you, but you make this people trust in a lie. Therefore thus says the LORD: 'Behold, I will cast you from the face of the earth. This year you shall die, because you have taught rebellion against the LORD.'" So Hananiah the prophet died the same year in the seventh month. (Jeremiah 28:15-17)

Some people do not believe the Lord would remove a person even if that person was deeply involved in rebellion. This is contrary to the Word of God in both the Old and New Testaments. Take a look at Jesus' letters to the seven churches in the second chapter of the book of Revelation. We are not in this world or this work alone. If your life and work are endangering the Lord's people and blocking His purposes, you are in danger of being removed. The prophet Hananiah did not repent and he died that very year. The one thing more dangerous than rebellion is teaching it to others.

Then the word of the LORD came to Jeremiah, saying: Send to all those in captivity, saying, Thus says the LORD concerning Shemaiah the Nehelamite: Because Shemaiah has prophesied to you, and I have not sent him, and he has caused you to trust in a lie—therefore thus says the LORD: Behold, I will punish Shemaiah the Nehelamite and his family: he shall not have anyone to dwell among this people, nor shall he see the good that I will do for My people, says the LORD, because

he has taught rebellion against the LORD.
(Jeremiah 29:30-32)

If you are in rebellion, you simply cannot carry the fire of God. It will consume you rather than being miscarried. Yet, there is so much rebellion in the church. As we travel and teach, we meet many pastors who have lost their church positions because of rebellion on the part of other church leaders and the people who follow them. Rebellious people cause so much disruption in the body of Christ when they act against the Lord's established authority. They cause revivals to end and church movements to stop. Many times we have gone back to places caught up in rebellion and we have seen that those who rebelled are no longer together. The groups they formed turned on each other and soon came to an end. The blessing and favor of the Lord will not be found in a rebellious group or a rebellious leader. I am being very blunt about this because it is true and I want to warn people about the danger to them, their families and their churches. Consider what the Lord said to King Saul through the prophet Samuel. We need to learn from these powerful lessons the Lord has given to us.

> *For rebellion is as the sin of witchcraft, and stubbornness is as iniquity and idolatry. Because you have rejected the word of the LORD, He also has rejected you from being king.* (1 Samuel 15:23)

Vision Report
Time is short

This morning, I was feeling the pressure of time restraints because we are leaving early for Moravian Falls. I was apologizing to the Lord for only spending a couple of hours with Him this morning and rushing to hear from heaven so I could send it out before we leave. I prayed that if my rush was a problem, I could wait to hear the word. Then He interrupted my thoughts by saying, "Don't waste any more time. If you understood how short the time is, you would not waste any more of it. There are serious choices that need to be made in these last days." I immediately remembered the words of Joshua to the people of Israel who were in a hurry to claim their share of the "promised land."

> *And if it seems evil to you to serve the Lord, choose for yourselves this day whom you will serve, whether the gods which your fathers served that were on the other side of the River, or the gods of the Amorites, in whose land you dwell. But as for me and my house, we will serve the Lord.* (Joshua 24:15)

There are many false God's in our world. Everywhere we look, there are people who are worshipping the creation instead of the creator. God is not being honored by our nations or most of our current world leaders. On many local levels, the church has allowed unrighteous leaders to take powerful political offices. These leaders have marginalized Christians and elevated almost every other religion to prominence. Every ethnic group and worldly philosophy is protected by unrighteous leaders and the true faith in God is being demonized in the entire culture. We need to hear the Joshua challenge again in our day. Choose this day for yourself whom you will serve. People are worshipping around things of the flesh and polluting themselves in spirit, soul, and body. We are in great peril and many have been lulled to sleep in this critical hour. Others are afraid to make waves because they do not want to be objects of the rampant and pervasive criticisms of this generation.

I am hearing the call of Joshua over and over. The Lord's people are being asked daily to make important decisions. Can you hear it? Chose this day whom you will serve. People today are giving so much of their time to the things that will not last. I see people walking around as if in a daze as they focus on their "smart phones" and tablets. They seem oblivious to their surroundings and unaware of the dangers so close at hand. Some just walk out into the street without ever looking up to assess the danger. So many young people are dying as they attempt to text and drive. People today seem so out of touch with reality. Even so, you are being asked to make a critically important decision today. Choose this day and every day whom you will serve.

It has never been enough to just choose for and to focus only on yourself. This is one of the worst forms of serving the flesh. We must choose this day to serve the Lord and the only way to truly serve Him is by sharing Him with as many other people as possible. We are to call as many as possible out of the darkness of doubt and deception into the light of the kingdom of the Son of His love. We are to bring enough light with us into the world to illuminate the kingdom of God for others to see. We should carry enough light to draw people to Him today. Study the passage below and decide how you will choose.

Do not love the world or the things in the world. If anyone loves the world, the love of the Father is not in him. For all that is in the world—the lust of the flesh, the lust of the eyes, and the pride of life—is not of the Father but is of the world. And the world is passing away, and the lust of it; but he who does the will of God abides forever. (1 John 2:15-17)

Time is short, and you can't afford to only spend it on yourself. There is a reckoning in our future. There is a day of judgment when the Lord will decide our eternal future. I want to dedicate all of my days on Earth to Him. How about you? I want to be faithful to His calling to spread the gospel of the kingdom and to light up all the dark places on earth before time runs out. Is this your calling? If it is, you must be aware of how little time is left. Think about what John taught about the shortness of time.

Little children, it is the last hour; and as you have heard that the Antichrist is coming, even now many antichrists have come, by which we know that it is the last hour. They went out from us, but they were not of us; for if they had been of us, they would have continued with us; but they went out that they might be made manifest, that none of them were of us. But you have an anointing from the Holy One, and you know all things. I have not written to you because you do not know the truth, but because you know it, and that no lie is of the truth. (1 John 2:18-21)

May you have an eternal focus from this day forward! May you discern the times and understand what you are to do for the kingdom of God! May you walk in the light and carry the light into the kingdom of darkness! May the Lord redeem all your remaining time to give it eternal significance! Amen!!!

(End of Vision Report)
PRAYER

Prayer is the key to carrying revival. Prayer is truly the foundation stone for revival. The righteous prayers of the Lord's people will bring revival. The righteous prayers of repentance will open the door for Holy Spirit fire and the Lord's power to win souls. During our trip to Wales, we learned that the great revival of 1904-1905 was firmly established on the prayers of the people which had been lifted up for several years before it manifested. May we be as resilient in our prayers for a great revival to come in our generation!

Holy Spirit come! Holy Spirit come and baptize us afresh with your fire so that we can carry the Lord's glory. Holy Spirit let your fire purify us from all those things which hinder revival and grieve your heart. Holy Spirit refine us as gold so that we can walk in holiness and carry your fire into the highways and byways of the places where we live and work. Holy Spirit forgive every tiny bit of rebellion and bitterness in our hearts. Remake us. Remold us. Let us be filled with a new zeal for evangelism and a new power to speak your words with fire and authority. Keep us humble and let us always be very careful to give you all the glory, honor and majesty which You so richly deserve. With humble hearts we submit to you. Receive us and release us to do the work you have assigned to us. We pray these things for your glory and for the advancement of the Kingdom. We pray these things in the mighty name of Yeshua ha Messiach. Amen and amen.

PAUSE AND REFLECT

1. What are the four things Jesus said would hinder our work for Him?

2. What are some additional things which may hinder revival?

3. What can you do if you see some of these characteristics in your own heart?

4. Why is rebellion so dangerous?

5. How can you get rid of every root of bitterness?

6. What is the potential price of pride and arrogance?

CHAPTER NINE

GOD IS A CONSUMING FIRE

VISION REPORT
CONSUMING FIRE

I was very slow moving this morning. I was moving somewhere between a Shabbat rest and pure laziness. I took longer than usual to complete my Bible study and to move upstairs to the worship room. Along the way, I decided to have a very long worship time this morning and just continue to enjoy this period of rest. However, the Lord had a different idea and I think you know which idea became manifest. As I was singing along with the words of "Open the Eyes of My Heart, Lord!" I was really focused on the verse, "I want to see Your Face!" While singing this, I dropped down on my knees and very shortly was face down before the Lord. Almost immediately, the Lord gave me a glorious vision.

I was standing on a hill looking out across a wide plain. A short distance (1-2 miles) in front of me was a mountain which came to a high peak (much higher than where I was standing). The distance between where I was standing and the mountain peak gave me a clear view of the top. The top of the mountain seemed to be on fire. As

I was caught up in looking at this scene, a word appeared near the foot of another mountain. In giant letters which seemed to be on fire was the word "ONE." Then other words appeared as I heard the Lord declare them in a voice filled with powerful authority. I saw in fiery letters, "The Lord your God is ONE!" This reminded me of the "Schma" written in Deuteronomy 6:4-5, *"Hear, O Israel: The Lord our God, the Lord is one! You shall love the Lord your God with all your heart, with all your soul, and with all your strength."*

As I continued to look in awe at this fiery vision, I heard the Lord command, "Stop worshipping other gods!" I wondered, "What other gods do we serve?" I heard the Spirit saying: "money, the flesh, selfish desires, and the world system." I thought, "Haven't we done that? Haven't we overcome these things to serve the Lord whole heartedly?" Then the word "HOLY!" appeared on the mountain. I was immediately reminded of the song I listen to every day: "Holy Unto You" by Joel Chernoff. One verse prays, "Make me kadosh l'chaim!" which means, I want to lead a life of holiness unto the Lord! I want to be set apart for the Lord! How about you?

Then it seemed as if the mountain in front of me exploded with fire like a volcano. I realized that this was not a vision of a volcano, but of the mountain of the Lord. What I saw was like the time when Moses and the Hebrew people stood before the Lord as He came down on the mountain in His fiery glory. The story is found in the nineteenth chapter of Exodus.

> *On the morning of the third day there was thunder and lightning, with a thick cloud over the mountain, and a very loud trumpet blast. Everyone in the camp trembled. Then Moses*

led the people out of the camp to meet with God, and they stood at the foot of the mountain. Mount Sinai was covered with smoke, because the LORD descended on it in fire. The smoke billowed up from it like smoke from a furnace, the whole mountain trembled violently, and the sound of the trumpet grew louder and louder. Then Moses spoke and the voice of God answered him. (Exodus 19:16-19, NIV):

This morning, I felt like I was there on that day and that I was seeing what they saw. It was awesome as I continued to watch. From the place where I was standing, I could see the consuming fire of God's presence. As we read in Exodus, the people below saw the smoke of the fire. I have longed to see some of the mighty acts of God which occurred in the past like this majestic scene of God's glory descending to meet His people. However, I knew that this was also about something which is going to happen again in the near future. The children of Israel were not ready for it. It caused them to tremble in fear and they refused to go up to meet with the Lord. Will it be like that for us? Will we fear the fiery glory of the Lord when it descends? Will we tremble and refuse to draw near to Him?

James 4:8 says, *"Draw near to God and He will draw near to you."* I really like this promise! How about you? However, most people are not too thrilled about the rest of this verse and verse 9, *"Cleanse your hands, you sinners; and purify your hearts, you double-minded. Lament and mourn and weep! Let your laughter be turned to mourning and your joy to gloom."* But there is hope! The good news is in verse 10, *"Humble yourselves in the sight of the Lord, and He will lift you up."* God always makes a way for us!

Hallelujah! Thank you Lord! Thank you for your calling on our lives! Thank you for calling us up on the Holy Mountain to meet with you! Thank you for covering us with the robe of Jesus' righteousness, a garment of praise which Jesus bestowed, and the blood of the Lamb! Going into God's presence like this is impossible for us, but with the Lord all things are possible. Trust Him today! Draw near to Him today! Enter into His rest today! Be refreshed, rested, and renewed today! Amen and Amen!

(End of Vision Report)

A CONSUMING FIRE

The sight of the glory of the Lord was like a consuming fire on the top of the mountain in the eyes of the children of Israel. (Exodus 24:17)

For the children of Israel, this was an early part of the Lord's self-revelation. Prior to their experience with Him on the mountain, little was actually known about the Lord. They had been told stories about the Lord's presence with the patriarchs Abraham, Isaac, and Jacob, but little was known about Him after that period of history until He sent a new prophet to them named Moses. It was difficult for them to believe what they were hearing from Moses, because they knew so little about the Lord. All that was about to change. They were in the midst of a progressive revelation like no one had experienced before. They began to see God differently. When they saw Him on the Mountain, they came to know Him as fire. This is what Moses taught them in Deuteronomy 4:24, *"For the Lord your God is a consuming fire, a jealous God."*

Later Moses led them through a time of remembrance. In the Hebrew language, the book of Deuteronomy was called *"Mishneh Torah"* which was commonly translated as the repetition of the Torah (teachings). It was seen as an explanation of the Torah given as a refresher course or summary in the last few weeks of Moses' life. Due to an unfortunate translation of the word Torah as law, many English speaking people think this is merely the second presentation of the law. The word Torah is better translated as teachings. When you understand this, it is easier to understand Deuteronomy as both a repetition and explanation of the teachings and principles the Lord gave to Moses on Mount Sinai. With this perspective look again at the passage below as if you are seeing it for the first time.

> *The Lord talked with you face to face on the mountain from the midst of the fire. I stood between the Lord and you at that time, to declare to you the word of the Lord; for you were afraid because of the fire, and you did not go up the mountain. He said: "I am the Lord your God who brought you out of the land of Egypt, out of the house of bondage. You shall have no other gods before Me."*
> (Deuteronomy 5:4-6)

Moses reminded the people of how the Lord appeared to them. They heard the voice of the Lord, but it was fire they saw with their eyes. The fire frightened them and they chose to withdraw from His presence. They saw a kind of power which was beyond human control. Most people want to have a god they can control through rituals, prayers and offerings. This is an illusion. Like a consuming fire, you cannot control or manipulate the Living God. The words the Lord spoke were as comforting as His appearance was frightening. He spoke to them as their savior and their redeemer. Then He made it clear that they could serve no other.

FIRE OF JUDGEMENT

The idea of an all-powerful God sounds good when you are in trouble and praying for help. You want the one who answers your prayers to be able to accomplish all He has promised and all you have asked. On the other hand, it can be intimidating to be standing before that God when you see Him as a consuming fire. People who know the uncleanness in their hearts can be unsettled in the presence of pure holiness and righteousness. Perhaps this fire would strike out at them. Their worst fears were realized when they saw His response to the rebellion led by a man named Korah. Read the passage below from their perspective as the fire of God comes forth as judgment on some rebellious leaders.

> *Now it came to pass, as he finished speaking all these words, that the ground split apart under them, and the earth opened its mouth and swallowed them up, with their households and all the men with Korah, with all their goods. So they and all those with them went down alive into the pit; the earth closed over them, and they perished from among the assembly. Then all Israel who were around them fled at their cry, for they said, "Lest the earth swallow us up also!" And a fire came out from the Lord and consumed the*

*two hundred and fifty men who were offering
incense.* (Numbers16:31-35)

You need a very active imagination to see these things
clearly and to take it all in. I like to make a mental image
of these mighty moves of God so that I too can experience the depth of their meaning and purpose. It is a challenge to picture a fire coming out from the presence of the
Lord and instantly consuming two hundred and fifty men.
After this, the remainder of the children of Israel knew and
understood what it meant when they called Him a consuming fire. The only thing left was the censors they had
been carrying. The censors were not harmed because
they were holy. Moses used this imagery to warn the
people about the judgment which would come for going
back to idolatry after all the Lord had done for them.

> *Take heed to yourselves, lest you forget the
> covenant of the LORD your God which He
> made with you, and make for yourselves a
> carved image in the form of anything which
> the LORD your God has forbidden you. For the
> LORD your God is a consuming fire, a jealous
> God.* (Deuteronomy 4:23-24)

The passages above describe the responses of the
children of Israel to the earlier parts of the Lord's self-disclosure. They quickly saw and understood the fire. It was
more easily understood than the positive attributes of the
Lord. The people went through many cycles of rebellion
and restoration. Each time they rejected the Lord, He with-
drew His protection and they were quickly overpowered
by other nations. When they repented and cried out to the
Lord, He rescued and restored them. This happened over

and over until eventually, they had to receive the lesson of the fire again.

> *Behold, the name of the Lord comes from afar, burning with His anger, and His burden is heavy; His lips are full of indignation, and His tongue like a devouring fire.* (Isaiah 30:27)

Notice how the psalmist described the Lord in Psalm 18:8, (NIV), "*Smoke rose from his nostrils; consuming fire came from his mouth, burning coals blazed out of it.*" We like to think we have matured since those days, but it doesn't take long to notice that the nations are once again in a cycle of disobedience and rebellion against the Lord. Can we expect the Lord to be like a benevolent old grandfather who overlooks all these things and fails to see the truth about the condition of the world? I don't think so. He is God and He will be glorified. Study the passage below and see how it applies to the nations of the world today.

> *The Lord will cause men to hear his majestic voice and will make them see his arm coming down with raging anger and consuming fire, with cloudburst, thunderstorm and hail.* (Isaiah 30:30, NIV)

FIRE AS PROTECTION

> *Therefore understand today that the* LORD *your God is He who goes over before you as a consuming fire. He will destroy them and bring them down before you; so you shall drive them out and destroy them quickly, as the* LORD *has said to you.* (Deuteronomy 9:3)

It is much easier to accept and appreciate God's fire as protection. The Torah is filled with references to God moving in this way on behalf of the children of Israel. For over forty years the children of Israel lived under the protective power of God and visibly saw that Pillar of Fire almost every night. It must have been comforting to see it take up a protective position between them and Egypt's pursuing army. Moses assured the people that the God of fire would go into the Promised Land ahead of them and drive their enemies out before them. Moses assured them that those people who chose to fight against Israel would face the fire of God.

Would you like the same assurance? If you would like this, then look closely at the promise released in the book of Hebrews. The same God who protected the children of Israel will protect you and me. He is still a consuming fire. We can take comfort in the knowledge that He is our protector. At the same time, we need to revere Him and have a *"godly fear"* toward Him. The writer cautions us to remember that He is still a consuming fire. It is still true that *"The fear of the* LORD *is the beginning of wisdom; a good understanding have all those who do His commandments." (Psalm111:10)* Consider these things as you study the passage below.

> *Therefore, since we are receiving a kingdom which cannot be shaken, let us have grace, by which we may serve God acceptably with reverence and godly fear. For our God is a consuming fire.* (Hebrews 12:28-29)

FIRE TO LEAD

Yet in Your manifold mercies You did not forsake them in the wilderness. The pillar of the cloud did not depart from them by day, to lead them on the road; nor the pillar of fire by night, to show them light, and the way they should go. (Nehemiah 9:19)

The children of Israel received the physical manifestation of a great spiritual reality. One of the main purposes of both the Holy Spirit and the fire is to lead. If you will allow Him to do His work in you and for you, He will guide you in both the natural realm and in the spiritual realm. When Nehemiah wrote this passage, he was looking back on the journey of his ancestors through the wilderness. His mental picture was of them traveling on a road. However, much of the road did not exist at that time. It was created by millions of feet moving across the wilderness. They couldn't follow an existing road. So they followed the pillar of fire at night and the cloud by day.

Perhaps the Lord is calling you to journey through some uncharted waters or along some wilderness way. It takes a great deal of faith to begin such a journey, and it takes even more to continue during the dark seasons. You can continue because you have a guide. The Lord sent the Holy Spirit and the fire to guide you as He guided the children of Israel. This was one of Jesus' promises as His earthly ministry came to a close. He was doing some faith building with His disciples when He gave the promise in the passage below. Let it build your faith right now. The promise is still good. You have a guide. Follow Him. Follow the fire! Amen?

I still have many things to say to you, but you cannot bear them now. However, when He, the Spirit of truth, has come, He will guide you into all truth; for He will not speak on His own authority, but whatever He hears He will speak; and He will tell you things to come. He will glorify Me, for He will take of what is Mine and declare it to you. (John 16:12-14)

Truth is a big topic, and you need a big helper to teach you what you need to know at any given moment. The Holy Spirit will not withhold anything you need, but He will only give you what you are prepared to receive. I pray for this promise almost daily. I need truth to move forward in this season of the Lord. I don't focus on my need for worldly truth as much as I pursue spiritual truth. This is the only truth which will reveal the presence, plans and purposes of the Lord for your life. Receive it by faith daily, and you will not get off of the Lord's pathway. He will keep you on the *"highway of holiness."*

FIRE TO GIVE LIGHT

Nehemiah identified an important function of the fire of the Lord which was given to the children of Israel. It came *"to show them light,"* and it will come to you for the same purpose and provide the same outcomes. We have a promise that we will one day have the same experience. (Revelation 21:23) *"The city had no need of the sun or of the moon to shine in it, for the glory of God illuminated it. The Lamb is its light."* These gifts of God coming to us on the earth are foreshadowing a better promise for the future. The glory of God and the glory of Yeshua ha Messiach will provide all the light we need.

I am writing this section very early in the morning. The sun has not yet risen. As I work on this manuscript, I need light to see the keyboard and to read sections in my Bibles. I am thankful this morning that I have electrical lights which allow me to see anytime of the day or night. The children of Israel had to do many things after the sun went down, and they needed light to do it safely. The pillar of fire provided that light. The Lord was taking care of their every need. This is a source of great comfort and assurance for you and me. As He took care of them, He will take care of us.

Do you need more light to see? I am always praying for more of the light of revelation so that I can see greater spiritual truths in the Word of God. He is faithful to give light. He has been doing it since the beginning of time and He will continue to provide for His people for all eternity. You can count on it because you know you can always count on Him. He is faithful to keep all His promises. Amen?

FIRE TO SHOW THE WAY

Nehemiah reminded the people of another purpose for the fire of God. In Moses' day, the pillar of fire showed them *"the way they should go."* Early in my time as an Army Chaplain, I spent lots of days and nights in the wilderness with soldiers. We often moved at night. There were several reasons for this. In the heat of the summer, it was much cooler to move at night and soldiers could endure longer movements. Another benefit was that it was more difficult for the enemy to see you. This allowed you to constantly surprise enemy forces.

At one time, I was stationed on a post which was located partially in Kentucky and partially in Tennessee. If you have been in the wilderness in these two states, you have probably experienced what we did. It was often so dark that you literally could not see your own hand in front of your face. It was a challenge to move through this heavily forested area without light. Our leaders ordered us to attach a very small strip of white tap on the back of our helmets. If you remained close to the person in front of you, you could just make out a light glow from the very limited available light reflecting from the tape. The safest route was to step where he stepped. I always marveled at the officers leading these groups. They seemed to be able to see in the darkness without any night vision equipment.

I follow the Holy Spirit in much the same way. I try to stay very close to Him so that I can step where He steps and turn where He turns. I may not be able to see the way to our objective, but He can. I marvel at His abilities and His willingness to lead. This same Holy Spirit is available to you. He is also a light for your path. You can trust Him and follow Him. He is the blazing Menorah John saw before the throne of God in Heaven. He is the fire which guides your path.

> And the LORD *went before them by day in a pillar of cloud to lead the way, and by night in a pillar of fire to give them light, so as to go by day and night. He did not take away the pillar of cloud by day or the pillar of fire by night from before the people.* (Exodus 13:21-22)

SPIRIT FOR PROVISION

> *You also gave Your good Spirit to instruct them, and did not withhold Your manna from their mouth, and gave them water for their thirst. Forty years You sustained them in the*

wilderness; they lacked nothing; their clothes did not wear out and their feet did not swell. (Nehemiah 9:20-21)

Nehemiah wanted to remind the people who were following him about what the Lord had done for their ancestors. He wanted them to understand that the Lord still takes care of His people with the same gifts, graces and powers. The presence of the Lord in the fire reminds us that the Lord is our provider. He constantly did supernatural things to bring food and water to His people. He even protected their clothes and shoes so that they didn't wear out and their feet didn't swell.

When large numbers of soldiers first deployed to the Middle East, they had to change from their wood-lawn battledress uniforms to desert camouflage. One of the things which really surprised them was how quickly their new boots were worn out. The people who designed and manufacture the boots evidently didn't test them in the desert. We all gained a new appreciation for footwear which could endure the harsh environment of the wilderness. This gave me a new appreciation for what the Lord provided to the children of Israel.

And Moses said to the Lord: "Then the Egyptians will hear it, for by Your might You brought these people up from among them, and they will tell it to the inhabitants of this land. They have heard that You, Lord, are among these people; that You, Lord, are seen face to face and Your cloud stands above them, and You go before them in a pillar of cloud by day and in a pillar of fire by night." (Numbers 14:13-14)

As the Lord provides for His people, it is a testimony for the nations about the nature of God. He is our provider and we can trust Him. Can you imagine the look on their faces when they heard that the children of Israel had a daily manifestation of the presence of God in a visible pillar of cloud by day and a pillar of fire by night? This would be very disconcerting for any enemy force. How can you go up against something like that? These signs and wonders became another source of provision for them. It was a source of protection released by their provider. You can be certain that He will also provide for you when you are faithfully following Him.

> *Now it came to pass, in the morning watch, that the LORD looked down upon the army of the Egyptians through the pillar of fire and cloud, and He troubled the army of the Egyptians. And He took off their chariot wheels, so that they drove them with difficulty; and the Egyptians said, "Let us flee from the face of Israel, for the LORD fights for them against the Egyptians."* (Exodus 14:24-25)

This manifestation of the Lord was very troubling for the Egyptian army. They were no longer fighting against flesh and blood. They had come up against the Lord himself, and they were powerless in the fight. Not only was this emotionally and spiritually troubling, it was also physically troubling. The Lord was causing the chariot wheels to fall off as they moved. The chariots which had given them an advantage before were now the source of trouble for them. The Lord turned their strength into a weakness and made it very difficult for them to move. This kind of provision will also be there for you as you follow Him. Remember Jesus' invitation:

> *Come to Me, all you who labor and are heavy laden, and I will give you rest. Take My yoke upon you and learn from Me, for I am gentle and lowly in heart, and you will find rest for your souls. For My yoke is easy and My burden is light.* (Matthew 11:28-30)

FIRE OF SALVATION

> *Moreover You led them by day with a cloudy pillar, and by night with a pillar of fire, to give them light on the road which they should travel.* (Nehemiah 9:12)

The Lord gave fire to His people for many purposes. One of those purposes was to save them from danger as they traveled. This foreshadowed a great kind of salvation which would come through the completed work of Yeshua ha Messiach. In the meantime, He gave fire to the priest so they could atone for the sins of the people. This most often happened during the seasonal sacrifices, but it also happened on other occasions when immediate action was needed.

> *So Moses said to Aaron, "Take a censer and put fire in it from the altar, put incense on it, and take it quickly to the congregation and make atonement for them; for wrath has gone out from the Lord. The plague has begun." Then Aaron took it as Moses commanded, and ran into the midst of the*

assembly; and already the plague had begun among the people. So he put in the incense and made atonement for the people. And he stood between the dead and the living; so the plague was stopped. (Numbers 16:46-48)

This passage of scripture reveals to us what is probably Aaron's finest moment in his years of service to the Lord. He took fire from the altar and put it in the censer of incense and ran right into the middle of an outbreak of death by plague. Literally standing on the line between life and death, he performed the ritual of atonement. This released the power of God to stop the plague. The fire and smoke of the burning incense released a covering from the Lord for the people. It foreshadowed what the blood of Jesus and the fire of the Holy Spirit would bring to us.

You and I are also priests in the Kingdom of God because of the finished work of Christ. Remember what the word says in Revelation 5:10 (NIV), "*You have made them to be a kingdom and priests to serve our God, and they will reign on the earth.*" Therefore, these promises are also for us. As led by the Holy Spirit, we can use the fire of God to bring others from the jaws of death into the kingdom of the Son of His love. It is our duty and privilege to serve as His hands and mouth to accomplish His purpose. We can also take great comfort knowing that He has already done this for you and for me.

NOT JUST OLD TESTAMENT

Some people look at these passages of scripture and believe that these are only stories about things which happened long ago but are not available now. I don't see it this way. Every promise of the Bible is for you and me right now. We just need to step up in faith and receive them. These accounts of the fire of God are not just Old Testament images. That is why the writer of the book of Hebrews could declare: "*For our God is a consuming fire.*" (Hebrews 12:29) The Lord is the same yesterday, today and forever. This is a forever promise. In the new heaven and the new earth, He will still be the consuming fire providing for us. Consider His promise released through the prophet Isaiah.

> *Then GOD will bring back the ancient pillar of cloud by day and the pillar of fire by night and mark Mount Zion and everyone in it with his glorious presence, his immense, protective presence, shade from the burning sun and shelter from the driving rain.* (Isaiah 4:5-6 TMSG)

This promise has not yet been fulfilled. I believe it will happen just as the Lord promised. We can look forward to another time when these powerful manifestations will come to the Lord's people. At that time, the Lord will do for us what He did for those who went through the wilderness with Moses. I am praying that we will not respond to Him as they did. I am praying that we will be ready to see, believe and receive all that His presence and fire will bring. We need to be building up our faith right now so we will be prepared for that season. As you read the passage below, let it build your trust in the Lord. Always remember that He keeps every promise.

> *Through the Lord's mercies we are not consumed, because His compassions fail not. They are new every morning; great is*

Your faithfulness. "The Lord is my portion,"
says my soul, "Therefore I hope in Him!"
(Lamentations 3:22-24)

Have you experienced the Lord this way in your life? I have and it assures me that I can trust Him in the future. We may go through some dark nights, but we can make it on the hope He provides. His mercies are new every morning. You may be going through some tough times right now and you may need this reassurance. Read it aloud over and over until it becomes yours. Store it in your heart and bring it out every time you go through the darkness. Speak aloud to the Lord right now and affirm: *"great is Your faithfulness."* Say it again. Then make another powerful affirmation: *"The Lord is my portion," says my soul, "Therefore I hope in Him!"*

The sinners in Zion are terrified; trembling
grips the godless: "Who of us can dwell with
the consuming fire? Who of us can dwell with
everlasting burning?" (Isaiah 33:14, NIV)

Isaiah raised some important questions. Who can dwell with consuming fire? Can you dwell with this everlasting burning? The only way you can do it is if you have already been through the fire. Seek the fire of God now while He is near. Seek to have your heart refined and purified to make you ready to live in His presence. Now is the time of your visitation. Today is the day of His salvation. Reach out for it now. Then you can be like the person Isaiah describes below.

He who walks righteously and speaks what
is right, who rejects gain from extortion and

keeps his hand from accepting bribes, who stops his ears against plots of murder and shuts his eyes against contemplating evil— this is the man who will dwell on the heights, whose refuge will be the mountain fortress. His bread will be supplied, and water will not fail him. (Isaiah 33:15-16, NIV)

BURNING BUSH AS A TYPE FOR US!

Now Moses was tending the flock of Jethro his father-in-law, the priest of Midian. And he led the flock to the back of the desert, and came to Horeb, the mountain of God. And the Angel of the Lord appeared to him in a flame of fire from the midst of a bush. So he looked, and behold, the bush was burning with fire, but the bush was not consumed. Then Moses said, "I will now turn aside and see this great sight, why the bush does not burn." So when the Lord saw that he turned aside to look, God called to him from the midst of the bush and said, "Moses, Moses!" And he said, "Here I am." Then He said, "Do not draw near this place. Take your sandals off your feet, for the place where you stand is holy ground." Moreover He said, "I am the God of your father—the God of Abraham, the God of Isaac, and the God of Jacob." And Moses hid his face, for he was afraid to look upon God. (Exodus 3:1-6)

In Moses' time, only a few were called to go up the mountain into the fire of God. They were on the other side of the cross and did not have the covering of Yeshua's blood. They had a temporary covering of the blood of animal sacrifices. They knew that it didn't last very long. They had to do it over and over, but it is not like that for you and me. We have the eternal offering of the blood of Yeshua ha Messiach. He has once and for all time provided a covering for our sin. Because of what He has done we can stand on holy ground.

We still need to stand in His presence with awe and respect. I do this symbolically by removing my shoes every time I walk into our worship room where the presence of God manifests so powerfully every day. I do this to show my awe and respect for His presence. He is still a consuming fire. He is still the provider. He is still as powerful as ever, and He deserves much more honor and glory than we are able to give. So, I try to give Him all I have each day. How about you? Think about some ways you can give Him the honor, glory and majesty He so richly deserves for all He has done for you, your family and your church. Amen?

PRAYER

Then you call on the name of your gods, and I will call on the name of the LORD; and the God who answers by fire, He is God. So all the people answered and said, "It is well spoken." (1 Kings 18:24)

Father, thank you for being the God who still answers by fire. Thank you for the fire you release in our lives through the presence of Your Holy Spirit. Thank you for always being with us to lead us and guide our steps along the old paths and the new ones you are revealing right now. Thank you for standing watch over us by fire so that our enemies will stay at a distance. Thank you for giving light to our spirits so that we can understand you more fully each day. Thank you for giving us Yeshua ha Messiach, the Holy Spirit and your Word to lead us through present day wildernesses. You are awesome and we love and honor you today and always in the mighty name of Yeshua ha Messiach. Amen and Amen!!!

PAUSE AND REFLECT

1. Describe one experience you have had with the fire of God.

2. How would you like for the fire of God to manifest in your ministry?

3. In what ways does the fire of God bring comfort to you?

4. What does it mean to you when you think of God as a consuming fire?

5. How can you go about receiving more fire from the Lord?

6. How can a human being dwell with consuming fire?

CHAPTER TEN

OUR GOD ANSWERS BY FIRE!

VISION REPORT
A RAGING FIRE

January 27, 2010 — Wednesday Morning at 7:30 a.m.

I n an early morning vision, I saw a giant raging fire. I was reminded by the Holy Spirit of the description of God in Hebrews 12:29, "for our "*God is a consuming fire.*" I immediately understood that the fire I was seeing was the Lord. His glory was like a raging fire. I knew in my spirit that He is indeed a consuming fire. As I watched, I saw that the fire was moving. As it moved it was consuming mountains along its path. These great stone formations were helpless before Him and easy work for the consuming fire of our God. I was in awe of His power, and amazed that He desires for fragile beings like you and me to draw close to His glory fire.

Then I was shown great billowing columns of smoke. Each of the columns was rising up to the heavens. I remembered how the Lord led Israel for all those years in the wilderness with columns of smoke. They must have looked something like what I was being shown. Each one rose up from the fiery presence of the Lord. Once again, I was in awe of the Lord. He is not limited to one column of smoke or just one people. He is the leader of all who will open their eyes to see and their ears to hear His voice.

Flashes of light from above began to pierce the clouds as they fell earthward. As they were hit by the light of His glory the mountain tops were shattered. The flashes of light became stronger and stronger. Now they appeared to be like great bolts of lightning. I felt so privileged to see this powerful display of the power of our God and Savior. I am growing more and more in the awe of the Lord and more and more amazed that He calls us to follow Him. He is the God who answers by fire, and like the people in the days of Elijah, I want to cry out, "The Lord – He is God! The Lord – He is God!" I pray that you are also experiencing the awesome nature as well as the powerful presence of the Lord in your life and ministry. I am praying that He is answering you with fire.

As I sought guidance from the Holy Spirit, I was told that many in the church are still searching for "little Jesus, meek and mild." I was told that this is a complete misunderstanding of who He is, what He does and how He will return. Remember what Jesus taught in Luke 21:27-28, *"Then they will see the Son of Man coming in a cloud with power and great glory. Now when these things begin to happen, look up and lift up your heads, because your redemption draws near."* We must be ever mindful of who He is and in awe of His power and glory.

Don't be deceived into a false image of the Lord. Be aware that many people are teaching manmade doctrines which are a complete misunderstanding of what it means to be kingdom minded even while living on earth. Think about what Jesus meant when He spoke in Matthew 11:12, *"And from the days of John the Baptist until now the kingdom of heaven suffers violence, and the violent take it by force.*" Kingdom minded people are not meek and weak either. They are the ones who are filled with an overwhelming hunger and thirst to be with the Lord. They will not be deterred from seeking His face and pressing into His Kingdom. Their rush to be with Him may even appear to be violent to the truly meek and weak among us.

Our God is an all-powerful God (a consuming fire) who is coming in great power and glory. He is the One who rewards all of those who seek His face. He blesses those who have so much hunger that it drives them to pursue Him with so much force that it could be described as violent. It is time to forcefully press in to the kingdom of God. It is time to be a part of bringing His kingdom on earth as it is in heaven. This will not be done with meekness and mildness, but in the mighty power of God. This is good news for those who love Him and seek him without regard to their personal cost. Those who seek Him with all their heart will find Him. In reality, they will be found by Him. Thanks be to God. Amen? Draw close now to the God who answers by fire! Amen?

(End of Vision Report)
ELIJAH WAS A FIRE FIGHTER

During my early development in the church, the Sunday School teachers primarily taught from the colorful Biblical stories of people like David, Elijah, Daniel, Shadrach, Meshach, and Abed-Nego. I loved those stories as a child and my faith in God was shaped by the points they taught through these Biblical references. These stories and the teachings revealed through them have remained with me through the years. It is likely that every child who attends Christian Education today also knows stories about God's heroes of the faith. Do you realize that these same stories were used to educate children and adults in Biblical times? They were told over and over around the campfires at night. The spiritual journey of each new generation began by hearing and understanding what the Lord could do with one life fully committed to Him. Study the Eleventh Chapter of the book of Hebrews to learn more about these mighty men and women of the Bible. Consider again the list provided below and be encouraged by them.

And what more shall I say? For the time would fail me to tell of Gideon and Barak and Samson and Jephthah, also of David and Samuel and the prophets: who through faith subdued kingdoms, worked righteousness, obtained promises, stopped the mouths of lions, quenched the violence of fire, escaped the edge of the sword, out of weakness were made strong, became valiant in battle, turned to flight the armies of the aliens. Women received their dead raised to life again. (Hebrews 11:32-35)

Children often grow up with stories of modern day heroes who risk everything to help others. One special type of first responder is looked up to by most children. They are the fire fighters of our day. Many children have an early desire to grow to be a fireman or firewoman. For most, these dreams are put aside somewhere along the way. Unfortunately this often happens when they learn how low the salaries are for our first responders. When money and the things of the flesh have more weight in our decision making than our childhood hopes and plans, many fiery dreams grow cold. Yet, even if these children give up their plans for this profession, most still hold them in high esteem.

As I studied the life and times of the prophet Elijah, I began to think of him as a fire fighter of a different sort. He didn't put fires out! He started them! As children, we may be taught about his battle with the prophets of Baal. The imagery of the Lord answering by fire is both vivid and instructive. We hope our children will learn from these teachings rather than by making the same mistakes as others in the past. Fire is a good teacher. We learn at an early age to respect fire because of the potential pain which comes from getting too close.

The Lord taught Elijah to fight the enemy with the fire of God. He fought the false prophets with FIRE. He gave a vivid and powerful challenge to the false prophets: "*Then you call on the name of your gods, and I will call on the name of the Lord; and the God who answers by fire, He is God.*" (1 Kings 18:24) This is risky business. Do you have enough faith to challenge the false teachers and false prophets of this day and time? The Lord proved Himself trustworthy in the life and ministry of the prophet Elijah. The God who answered by fire was the living creator God. The winner of the contest was the God of Elijah. The results were amazing. 1 Kings 18:39 (NIV), "*When all the people saw this, they fell prostrate and cried, 'The LORD—he is God! The LORD—he is God!'*"

Sometimes it is necessary for the Lord to teach these lessons to adults again. They either forget or discount the lessons of the Bible somewhere along the way. As they grow up many people put their service to the Lord aside as do the children who want to become fire fighters. We are living in a time when many political and church leaders show little respect for Father God. He has been barred from schools, sports, and even some churches. Perhaps it is time to learn the lessons taught through Elijah's ministry again. Remember: He fought enemy armies with FIRE.

In one account, we see that it took three times at bat for them to learn to respect the fire and the God who answers by fire. Think about that as you study the passage below. It was bad enough for the first leader to fail so miserably, but what about that second one. It seems that he learned nothing from what the first group had experienced. Repetition is sometimes needed for lessons to be learned.

> *At this the king sent to Elijah another captain with his fifty men. The captain said to him, "Man of God, this is what the king says, 'Come down at once!'" "If I am a man of God," Elijah replied, "may fire come down from heaven and consume you and your fifty men!" Then the fire of God fell from heaven and consumed him and his fifty men."* (2 Kings 1:11-12)

The first two captains were arrogant and insensitive. They could not be trusted to take Elijah safely to the king. The second captain was more arrogant than the first, because he saw what happened to the first captain and yet did the same thing. He got the same results as the first one. The Lord resists the proud but blesses and lifts up the humble. The third captain was humble and did not suffer as the first two. Here is a powerful spiritual truth: humble and trustworthy leaders are blessed.

WHO DO YOU SERVE?

Do you know and serve the God Who answers by FIRE? This is the truly important point of this account.

God's show of power demanded a decision from the people that day, and it still calls for a decision today. The Lord is using these stories once again to call for a decision on your part. Whom will you choose to serve? I remind you today that this is a question which has been around for a very long time. Joshua challenged the children of Israel with this question as they moved into their promise land. Read Joshua 24:15 aloud, and make your decree like Joshua made his.

Our God speaks to us from the fire! He spoke to Elijah at the end of a firefight. The reason for this is made clear in 2 Kings 1:15. *"The angel of the Lord said to Elijah, "Go down with him; do not be afraid of him." So Elijah got up and went down with him to the king."* The Lord was protecting him from the enemy. He will also protect you. Sometimes you have to stand strong through the fight in order to see the end results. Don't be afraid of the Lord's fire. If you belong to Yeshua ha Messiah, the God who answers by fire is on your side.

Our God protects us in many ways and with many different weapons of both natural and spiritual warfare. In the Bible we see the Lord protecting His own with power, with fire, and with His Word! What about you? Are you moving in God's power? In the book of James, we are reminded that all these things are for us too. The Lord didn't just do this once for one special person. He came to the aid of His people over and over and demonstrated His power to believers and non-believers alike. Study the passage below. Read it aloud until it becomes yours. Then stand in faith and be as strong and effective as Elijah.

> *Elijah was a man with a nature like ours, and he prayed earnestly that it would not rain; and it did not rain on the land for three years*

and six months. And he prayed again, and the heaven gave rain, and the earth produced its fruit. (James 5:17-18)

MOSES WAS A FIREFIGHTER

When a group of rebels tried to usurp the authority of Moses and Aaron, they didn't have to fight in the normal human way. They didn't enter into a great theological debate about the nature of authority and holiness. They didn't protest or argue about Korah's false representation of their calling. They fell face down before the Lord in humility and submission and let the Lord take care of them. The Lord gave a very graphic lesson to the rebels by opening the ground under them so that they were buried alive. In addition to the leaders falling into the pit, fire came from the altar of God and consumed the 250 Levites who were making an illegal grab for the priesthood. They were approaching the altar with unauthorized fire and it backfired on them. The Lord had warned them not to approach the Holy place and Most Holy place without His invitation and authorization, but they didn't listen.

This was not the only time that the Lord released fire from the altar. Once before, He had released fire to protect the holiness of the service of the priesthood. Perhaps the rebels had forgotten this powerful visual lesson. Fire came from the altar and killed Aaron's two unholy sons. They mistakenly thought that any kind of fire was good enough for the Lord. So they made an offering of fire like the pagans did in their idol worship. This was a major violation of the Lord's commands. The Lord had given very precise instructions. Tragically the two sons of Aaron had been drinking and casually conducted the holy service in a profane manner. The key was not the fire. The key was obedience. It had been made clear that just any old fire would not work! It is the fire of God which will do the work of the Lord.

When Solomon finished praying, fire came down from heaven and consumed the burnt offering and the sacrifices, and the glory of the LORD filled the temple. The priests could not enter the temple of the LORD because the glory of the LORD filled it. When all the Israelites saw the fire coming down and the glory of the LORD above the temple, they knelt on the pavement with their faces to the ground, and they worshiped and gave thanks to the LORD, saying, "He is good; his love endures forever." (2 Chronicles 7:1-3)

ABRAHAM WAS A FIRE STARTER

And behold, the word of the Lord came to him, saying, "This one shall not be your heir, but one who will come from your own body shall be your heir." Then He brought him outside and said, "Look now toward heaven, and count the stars if you are able to number them." And He said to him, "So shall your descendants be." And he believed in the Lord, and He accounted it to him for righteousness. Then He said to him, "I am the Lord, who brought you out of Ur of the Chaldeans, to give you this land to inherit it." And he said, "Lord God, how shall I know that I will inherit it?" (Genesis 15:4-8)

Abram wanted to be certain about God's plan for him. He had already affirmed his belief (trust) in the Lord. His faith had already been accounted to him as righteousness, but there was this little nagging desire for more certainty. He just couldn't accept the Lord's spoken word alone. He needed some hard evidence as the foundation for the rest of his life. He believed. He had faith, but he still wanted assurance.

The Lord didn't chastise Abram. He set out to demonstrate visually, that His promise was certain. Abraham would go through some very trying times fulfilling his destiny from the Lord, and he was given a powerful visual image to keep him going through the dark days ahead. The Lord had him to prepare a sacrifice, but not to light the fire. Genesis 15:17 (NIV), "*When the sun had set and darkness had fallen, a smoking firepot with a blazing torch appeared and passed between the pieces.*" The Lord gave him two testimonies by fire. He had both a smoking firepot and a blazing torch manifest for a confirmation. Abraham fought his fears and concerns with the fire of God.

JESUS WANTED TO START A FIRE

> *I have come to bring fire on the earth, and how I wish it were already kindled! But I have a baptism to undergo, and what constraint I am under until it is completed! Do you think I came to bring peace on earth? No, I tell you, but division.* (Luke 12:49-51, NIV)

The coming time of judgment was often pictured as the kindling of a fire. There are numerous passages throughout the Old Testament speaking of the kindling of fire. This type of judgment was prophesied by the Lord through Isaiah, Jeremiah, Ezekiel, Amos, and Obadiah.

The day of this kindling is still coming in the future. The time of grace will soon pass and the time of judgment will be upon us. At that time the Lord will kindle that fire for the final time. We need to always be alert and ready for that time. We must seek to be ready to meet the Lord on that day. Remember: He is the God who answered by fire and we will one day see Him answer again in the same way.

In the meantime, another kind of fire was kindled. The Lord kindled a fire of baptism for the disciples on the Day of Pentecost. "*Then there appeared to them divided tongues, as of fire, and one sat upon each of them. And they were all filled with the Holy Spirit and began to speak with other tongues, as the Spirit gave them utterance.*" (Acts 2:3-4) Perhaps you need to have that Holy Spirit fire kindled over you right now. Ask the Lord. He gives to those who ask. Perhaps you need to have a fire kindled once more because one previously given by the Lord has grown cold. Again seek and you shall find. Ask and it will be given. Amen?

We are on a mission for the Lord. We need His power to accomplish it. On our own we will never have enough power or fire to accomplish the mission. Remember the old Missionary saying, "Where the Lord doth guide, the Lord doth provide." Do you believe that? I believe it. I expect it. I receive it by faith right now and give Him praise and thanksgiving for His faithfulness. I am fully confident that on the day when fire is needed, fire will be provided. How about you? Remember you have the same nature as Elijah. He fought with fire and so can you. You can do the things Elijah did. You can even do the things the Lord did. In addition, He has promised that you will be able to do even greater things. Remember the promise.

> *Most assuredly, I say to you, he who believes in Me, the works that I do he will do also; and*

greater works than these he will do, because I go to My Father. And whatever you ask in My name, that I will do, that the Father may be glorified in the Son. If you ask anything in My name, I will do it. (John 14:12-14)

Read these words of the Lord aloud over and over until they are yours. Then continue to read them and speak them regularly. This will build your faith for the hour when it is needed. I remind you again of the Lord's promise released by Paul in Romans 10:17, "*So then faith comes by hearing, and hearing by the word of God.*" This is the secret for turning your hopes into faith and your faith into action. This is the way to build up your faith so that you too can fight with the fire of God. Let it now burn up all doubt and unbelief. Let it put the fire of God in your belly and in your bones so that you have no choice except to release the gospel of the Kingdom with power and with signs and wonders following. Amen?

KINDLING THE FIRE IS YOUR TASK.

On the cross, Jesus declared, "*It is finished!*" His work is finished, but ours has only just begun. Jesus carried the fire and the power of God in His ministry. He passed it on to you and me. He released to us the same glory which the Father had given to Him. He released to us the same love that the Father had for Him. We have everything we need. So, it is time to put it all into action. Jeremiah could not hide the fire in his bones. He had to release it. The same is true for us. We cannot hide the fire or the light of God. These powerful gifts are given so that we can let them shine into the darkness and bring the lost back to the Lord.

No one lights a lamp and puts it in a place where it will be hidden, or under a bowl. Instead they put it on its stand, so that those who come in may see the light. Your eye is the lamp of your body. When your eyes are healthy, your whole body also is full of light. But when they are unhealthy, your body also is full of darkness. See to it, then, that the light within you is not darkness. Therefore, if your whole body is full of light, and no part of it dark, it will be just as full of light as when a lamp shines its light on you. (Luke 11:33-36, NIV)

It is always good to begin with some introspection. What kind of light is in you now? What kind of fire are you carrying? Jesus said that the light of many people is actually darkness! What about the light which is in you? Remember what He commanded, "*See to it, then, that the light within you is not darkness.*" (Luke 11:35, NIV) If your light has grown dim or if the fire is about to go out, you need to take action right now. It is a time to repent and to be restored. It is a good time to return to the Lord. Remember the process this way: Repent – restore – return.

On the other hand, if the light in you is the light of God, let it shine! If the fire in you is the fire of God, let it burn with blazing intensity. Remember the image of the Holy Spirit given in Revelation 4:5 (NIV), "*From the throne came flashes of lightning, rumblings and peals of thunder. Before the throne, seven lamps were blazing. These are the seven spirits of God.*" When you receive the Holy Spirit baptism this blazing fire comes to you. It comes on you and it comes into you. Now is the time to be on fire for the Lord. Time is short and we have many fires to kindle.

DON'T HIDE GOD'S LIGHT

You are the light of the world. A city that is set on a hill cannot be hidden. Nor do they light a lamp and put it under a basket, but on a lampstand, and it gives light to all who are in the house. Let your light so shine before men, that they may see your good works and glorify your Father in heaven. (Matthew 5:14-16)

YOUR LIGHT CAN BRING GLORY TO GOD!

Think about it. Jesus gave us a wonderful promise! He said that you and I can bring glory to Father God. This is an awesome thought and a holy responsibility. We need to live and minister in ways which bring glory to Him. I don't think that a powerless life with no Holy Spirit fire can possibly bring glory to Him. I don't think that weak and helpless disciples under constant attack bring glory to Father God. It is His empowered disciples, on fire for the gospel, who bring Him glory. Amen?

So what can you do? Shine the light of God which is in you so that others can see. Shine the light so they can find their way home. Shine your light toward God so others will see His presence and be drawn to Him! People are drawn to the winners and heroes in life. The Lord has commissioned you to be a winner so that you will become a role model for others to follow. He has released His light on you and in you for this very purpose. Always be aware that He is shining His light through you to accomplish His purposes.

Let Him do His amazing work through your life and ministry. 1 John 4:4, "*You are of God, little children, and have overcome them, because He who is in you is greater than he who is in the world.*" You are destined to be a victor. Your destiny is to march in a big victory parade at the end of the age. Right now your responsibility is to inspire others to trust the Lord. Now is the time to encourage people to give their lives to Him in the hour of their visitation and on the day of their salvation.

None of these things will happen if you hide your light! The Lord never meant for you to be a spot of dullness in a bright world. His plan is the opposite of this. He has planned to shine a bright light through you to break up the darkness of the world. Let this be the beginning of a brand new day. Let it be a new episode in your life of victory. Let you light shine in the darkness!

BECOME THE MIGHTY BLAZING FIRE OF GOD!

> *But you are a chosen people, a royal priesthood, a holy nation, God's special possession, that you may declare the praises of him who called you out of darkness into his wonderful light.* (1 Peter 2:9)

PRAYER

> *Therefore we also pray always for you that our God would count you worthy of this calling, and fulfill all the good pleasure of His goodness and the work of faith with power, that the name of our Lord Jesus Christ may be glorified in you, and you in Him, according to the grace of our God and the Lord Jesus Christ.* (2 Thessalonians 1:11-12)

PAUSE AND REFLECT

1. How can you use the fire of God in your ministry?

2. Describe an experience you have had using the fire of God.

3. How can you learn to fight with fire?

4. Do you know the God who answers by fire? How has this knowledge helped you?

5. What kind of fire did Jesus want to kindle?

6. What is the Lord saying to you about fire?

CHAPTER ELEVEN

GOD LOVES TO START FIRES

As you have read in the previous chapters, the Bible records many instances of God starting fires. I encourage you to go on an investigative journey of your own into the reality of the fire of God. Remember the Lord's promise in Revelation 21:5, "*Behold, I make all things new.*" Do you believe that? If you do, then you should always expect new things from the Lord. Even now, expect a fresh anointing of fire on you and your ministry. Expect the Lord to call on you to carry His fire to others.

Think of all the ways in which the Lord moves with fire. You already know all or most of these from your own training and study. At the end of this chapter, you will find a page with questions. Use some of this space to record additional aspects of the Lord's fire which you have experienced. We will begin this chapter with a quick review of some of the primary methods used by the Lord.

THE LORD'S USE OF FIRE
1. FIRE OF JUDGEMENT:

And I will make you cross over with your enemies into a land which you do not know; for

*a fire is kindled in My anger, which shall burn
upon you.* (Jeremiah 15:14)

Sometimes He kindles a fire of judgment. You can
clearly see this in the books of Isaiah, Jeremiah, Ezekiel,
and several of the lesser prophets. The Lord never does
this capriciously or without warning. He doesn't just get
angry and strike out at His people. He patiently waits for
them to respond to call after call and prophetic word after
prophetic word. His desire is for people to repent and
return to Him. He is long suffering, patient and merciful
beyond any human measure. When people continue to
refuse to repent and continue to hurt other people, His
patience will eventually run out. The Lord described it
this way in Jeremiah 17:27, *"But if you will not heed Me
to hallow the Sabbath day, such as not carrying a burden
when entering the gates of Jerusalem on the Sabbath day,
then I will kindle a fire in its gates, and it shall devour the
palaces of Jerusalem, and it shall not be quenched."*
When the people did not heed His word for extended
periods of time, He eventually held them accountable. Yet
in the midst of the fires of judgment, the Lord released
promises of His help and offered His mercy if they would
simply return to Him. Throughout the Bible, the Lord challenges the people to obey. Any nation which will repent
and return to the Lord will be saved from the coming judgment. The Lord will immediately respond to any people or
nation which will turn back to Him. Think about that when
you hear prophesies of judgment. Consider what the Lord
is saying to you in the passage below.

*When I shut up heaven and there is no rain,
or command the locusts to devour the land,
or send pestilence among My people, if*

My people who are called by My name will humble themselves, and pray and seek My face, and turn from their wicked ways, then I will hear from heaven, and will forgive their sin and heal their land. Now My eyes will be open and My ears attentive to prayer made in this place. (2 Chronicles 7:13-15)

It is good to have a heart to repent and return to the Lord. His promise is that He will relent from sending the promised judgment and restore His people. Note carefully that the Lord is looking for people who will obey instantly. It is that first response which touches the Lord's heart, and He always rewards and blesses those who are faithful. We must be prepared to turn quickly to Him when the fires of judgment are being released.

The instant I speak concerning a nation and concerning a kingdom, to pluck up, to pull down, and to destroy it, if that nation against whom I have spoken turns from its evil, I will relent of the disaster that I thought to bring upon it. And the instant I speak concerning a nation and concerning a kingdom, to build and to plant it, if it does evil in My sight so that it does not obey My voice, then I will relent concerning the good with which I said I would benefit it. (Jeremiah 18:7-10)

2. FIRE OF REVIVAL

Return, we beseech You, O God of hosts; look down from heaven and see, and visit this vine and the vineyard which Your right hand has planted, and the branch that You made strong for Yourself. It is burned with fire, it is cut down; they perish at the rebuke of Your countenance. Let Your hand be upon the man of Your right hand, upon the son of man whom You made strong for Yourself. Then we will not turn back from You; revive us, and we will call upon Your name. Restore us, O LORD God of hosts; cause Your face to shine, and we shall be saved! (Psalm 80:14-19)

Sometimes the Lord starts a fire to bring revival and restoration. He certainly did this during the reigns of King Josiah and King Hezekiah. They were both inspired to bring reform to the nation of Judah. They sought with all their hearts to return to a pure worship of the Lord and led their nation to rise again. It happened during the governor-ship of Nehemiah as he and the priest Ezra sought to bring the people back to the Lord. You can see over and over in these accounts and many others that the Lord is faithful to keep His Word. He promises that as people draw near to Him He will draw near to them. These promises were restated for you and me by James, the head of the church in Jerusalem and the brother of Yeshua ha Messiach. I encourage you to read it again in James 4:7-10.

On the day of Pentecost, the fire bringing revival fell on one hundred and twenty of Yeshua's followers who had gathered in the upper room. Thousands responded to the Lord's invitation to draw near and were saved on the days following this outpouring of the Holy Spirit and fire. I am so hungry for that to happen again. How about you? I am crying out for a fresh anointing of the Holy Spirit and for more fire daily.

As I was writing this section, someone sent a link to worship programs from the Lakeland Florida revival in 2008. As I thought about these things and listened to the worship, I was caught up again in the power and presence of the Lord as I had been during the twelve days my wife and I spent in that revival. It was like being translated back to that time and I was filled with joy. During this time of worship, I felt an overwhelming sense of hunger for another outpouring. I am crying out for something even greater than we experienced in Florida. I am so hungry and so thirsty for more of God. I am praying for an outpouring like the Welsh revival of 1904-1905 which will bring another great enlightenment and win thousands of lost souls for the Lord.

If you have never experienced this, I am praying for a mighty outpouring for you right now. If you get word of an outpouring of the power and presence, do whatever it takes to get yourself to that place and be a part of it. These gifts and graces will fall on you when you receive the baptism of the Holy Spirit and fire. Seek it with all your heart. If you have experienced it in the past, you know you are hungry for more. The more you drink of the living water, the more you thirst for it. The more the fire of God falls on you the more you desire it. We must never quit pressing in for more. My prayer for you right now is from Psalm 115.

May the Lord give you increase more and more, you and your children. May you be blessed by the Lord, Who made heaven and earth. The heaven, even the heavens, are the Lord's; But the earth He has given to the children of men. The dead do not praise the Lord, nor any who go down into silence. But we will bless the Lord from this time forth and forevermore. Praise the Lord! (Psalm 115-14-18)

David knew how to touch the heart of God. In His prayers, we can learn how to approach the Lord and make a connection which will bring restoration to our souls, salvation to our nation, and revival to our churches. Study the prayers of David and develop habits which will touch the Heart of God. Remember the description of David given in Acts 13:22, "*He raised up for them David as king, to whom also He gave testimony and said, 'I have found David the son of Jesse, a man after My own heart, who will do all My will.'*" Would you like to have this said about you? Then begin to practice the presence of God as David did. This is a good time to pray for revival and restoration in the same words as this mighty man of God.

Restore us, O God of our salvation, and cause Your anger toward us to cease. Will You be angry with us forever? Will You prolong Your anger to all generations? Will You not revive us again, that Your people may rejoice in You? Show us Your mercy, LORD, and grant us Your salvation. (Psalm 85:4-7)

3. FIRE AS APPROVAL

So David gave Ornan six hundred shekels of gold by weight for the place. And David built there an altar to the Lord, and offered burnt offerings and peace offerings, and called on the Lord; and He answered him from heaven by fire on the altar of burnt offering. (1 Chronicles 21:25-26)

Sometimes fire comes to show the Lord's approval. In the passage above, the Lord let David know that his offering had been accepted. He demonstrated His approved of the sacrifices with the release of His fire from heaven. As I thought about this, I began to cry out again for the fire of God to fall on our offerings of service, praise, worship and love for Him. I am crying out for Him to demonstrate His approval of what we are doing by sending fire from Heaven. Will you join with me in these prayers? I am so hungry for more fire.

The Lord did the same thing to show that He approved of the construction of the Tabernacle and Temple. They prepared the sacrifices, and the Lord provided the fire. He did the same thing for them that He would later do for Elijah. Remember that you have a nature like Elijah and you should develop the kind of faith which will bring Elijah sized results. In fact, you should have faith for more. Didn't Jesus tell you to expect to do "even greater things?" Think about it. What kind of fire are you seeking?

4. FIRE IN ANSWER TO PRAYER

When Solomon had finished praying, fire came down from heaven and consumed the burnt offering and the sacrifices; and the glory of the Lord filled the temple. And the priests could not enter the house of the Lord, because the glory of the Lord had filled the Lord's house. When all the children of Israel saw how the fire came down, and the glory of the Lord on the temple, they bowed their faces to the ground on the pavement, and worshiped and praised the Lord, saying: "For

He is good, for His mercy endures forever."
(2 Chronicles 7:1-3)

The Lord sent fire in answer to the prayers of His people. I wonder about our prayers today. Are you bringing down the fire of God with your prayers? If not, what must you do to rekindle the fire of God in your heart and your ministry? I am no longer content to just do business as usual. I am no longer content to do rituals on certain days without any sign of the Lord's fire. I can't do that anymore. I have experienced the fire of God and nothing less will do.

Lord help us to pray the kind of prayers that bring down your fire. We are no longer satisfied to just do church as usual. We have tasted the good things of your spirit, and we cannot accept anything less. We do not want to turn away. We want to continue to turn toward you. We cry out for you, the consuming fire, to draw near to us as we draw near. Let your fire burn away everything that hinders and everything which is not of you so that we can be in your Presence and your fire.

> *When the sun had set and darkness had fallen, a smoking firepot with a blazing torch appeared and passed between the pieces. On that day the LORD made a covenant with Abram and said, "To your descendants I give this land, from the river of Egypt to the great river, the Euphrates"* (Genesis 15:17-18, NIV)

The Lord sent fire on Abram's offering. Many people ask for the same kind of sign of His approval, but they must understand what they are asking for. The fire which fell on Abraham was a covenant making fire. If you are not ready to enter into a new and deeper covenant with the Lord, you may not want to ask for more fire. I want to move into a deeper intimacy with the consuming fire. How about you? If you are seeking this, pray with me. Father God, we are looking for another covenant making outbreak of fire. Purify us. Refine us. Make us ready to be in the presence of your fire and your glory.

When Moses and Aaron presented the offerings of the people, He sent such a powerful fire from His presence that it literally consumed the offering. The Lord received it all. He took it all. It was acceptable. His fire was their confirmation that they had done everything correctly. After the fire fell, they knew that they could operate in His presence and not fear death.

> *And Moses and Aaron went into the tabernacle of meeting, and came out and blessed the people. Then the glory of the Lord appeared to all the people, and fire came out from before the Lord and consumed the burnt offering and the fat on the altar. When all the people saw it, they shouted and fell on their faces.* (Leviticus 9:23-24)

They were to keep that fire of God burning night and day forever. As they journeyed from place to place, someone had to carry the fire. This was a holy calling and a very holy honor. How would you like to be responsible for keeping the Lord's fire burning? How would you like to be held accountable if you let the fire go out? How can you start this kind of fire again? The truth is that we cannot start the Lord's fire, but we can be faithful to carry it as we go in His Name. When God lights a fire for you, you must be careful to keep it burning. Think of all the revival fires which have gone out because some person failed to keep it going.

> *And the fire on the altar shall be kept burning on it; it shall not be put out. And the priest shall burn wood on it every morning, and lay the burnt offering in order on it; and he shall burn on it the fat of the peace offerings. A fire shall always be burning on the altar; it shall never go out.* (Leviticus 6:12-13)

The Lord spoke this command over and over. Remember what it means when the Lord says something twice. According to Joseph, when the Lord repeats something, it means that it is established. We must never let the fire of God go out in our hearts or in our ministries. It is your God-given task to keep the fire burning and to carry it out to His people.

The Lord answered David with fire when he repented and gave an offering on the altar he built on the threshing floor of Araunah. He had made a mistake in judgment. He had lapsed for a moment in his trust for the Lord. He looked to his mighty army for security and wanted to know exactly how large it was. For a moment, David forgot that it isn't the size of the army but the size of the Lord which brings victory. When he admitted his mistake and returned to the Lord, he got the answer he desired as fire came out from the Lord showing His acceptance. (see 1 Chronicles 21:25-26)

At the beginning of this section, you read 2 Chronicles 7:1-3. I encourage you to read it again. This is how the Lord answered Solomon's prayer at the dedication of the Temple. He sent fire on the altar. Over centuries of disobedience and rebellion, the fire on the altar of the Tabernacle had gone out. The people were far away from the Lord when Solomon enlisted them to help build the Temple.

They had high hopes that the glory of the Lord would return to their presence in His new dwelling. The Lord fulfilled all their hopes and dreams by lighting the fire again. His glory returned and the cloud of His Presence once again filled the Holy Place. It was so powerful that the priests could not minister. The people responded by falling on their faces in worship and praise. They declared again the ancient worship of a sincere heart when they cried out: *For He is good, for His mercy endures forever."*

In a latter generation when the people had fallen away again, the fire on the altar had gone out. The light of His glory was no longer in their midst. The glory days were gone and they only knew of them from the stories told by the elders. Then Elijah stepped forward with a courageous challenge. With no evidence but his faith, he declared that the God who answers by fire it the true God of Israel. Would you have the courage to make such an audacious claim?

It is time for the Lord's people to rise up again in the strength of their faith. It is time for the Lord's people to challenge the false gods and false teaching in this age. It is time to decree and expect to see the fire of God coming again. The Lord sent fire on Elijah's offering. We are told in scripture that Elijah was like us in his nature. This statement is clearly implying that we can do what he did. As you read the passage below, put yourself in Elijah's shoes and build your faith in order to carry and release the fire of God. 1 Kings 18:24, *"Then you call on the name of your gods, and I will call on the name of the Lord; and the God who answers by fire, He is God. So all the people answered and said, 'It is well spoken.'"*

The people all agreed to let this be their test of faith. Perhaps they had very little faith that it would actually happen. They may have felt the chances were very remote and they were safe in making this assumption. Whatever motivated them, they had set the stage for one of the greatest outpourings of God's fire recorded in the Bible. To prove his point, Elijah insisted that they pour water on the sacrifice in such abundance that it ran down and filled the trench around the altar. This made the demonstration of God's power much more dramatic and awe inspiring. Try to picture it in your own mind as you read the passage below.

> *Then the fire of the Lord fell and consumed the burnt sacrifice, and the wood and the stones and the dust, and it licked up the water that was in the trench. Now when all the people saw it, they fell on their faces; and they said, "The Lord, He is God! The Lord, He is God!" (1 Kings 18:38-39)*

5. FIRE DESTROYS THE ENEMY

Sometimes the fire of God comes to destroy His enemies. We saw that earlier with the fate which befell the 250 followers of Korah. As they presented unauthorized fire before the Lord, they were hit by such a powerful blast of fire that they were totally consumed. Rebellion can seem strong when the number of rebels increases, but their power is miniscule compared to the fire of God. Tragically, the people didn't learn from this powerful visual aid. They rebelled again the very next day.

Some people try to make a distinction between the God of the Old Testament and the Lord of the New Testament.

Some try to convince people that God will never use His fire in judgment against sinful mankind. Think about this: God is the same in both the Old Testament and New Testament. Remember Hebrews 13:8, "*Jesus Christ is the same yesterday, today, and forever.*" God has not changed and He will not change to adapt to our manmade ideas and doctrines. As you study the passage below, you will see that God has not changed.

> *They went up on the breadth of the earth and surrounded the camp of the saints and the beloved city. And fire came down from God out of heaven and devoured them. The devil, who deceived them, was cast into the lake of fire and brimstone where the beast and the false prophet are. And they will be tormented day and night forever and ever.*
> (Revelation 20:9-10)

We are assured in the book of Revelation, that the fire of God will destroy the massive army which comes against the Lord in the last days. The soon and coming King of kings and Lord of lords will not be a pushover for popular but totally unbiblical ideas about the person and nature of God. He is merciful, kind, loving and long suffering, but He is also the God of justice and righteousness. God will never tolerate the errors, violence and sin of one person when it brings harm to others. That would not be love at all.

There is no difference between the God pictured in the Book of Revelation and the God who was with the prophet Elijah. He is the same God. He is still a consuming fire. He is still powerful, just and righteous. He will not tolerantly sit by while people rise up to do harm to His prophets.

Government leaders today would be wise to heed these truths from the Word. Consider what happened when merciless and uncaring men were sent to arrest Elijah. (see 2 Kings 1:9-12)

FAITH TO FIGHT WITH FIRE

In both the Old and New Testaments we see that God at times fights with fire. If we are created in His image, should we at times fight with fire? If we are to be like Yeshua ha Messiach, is there a season in which we carry and use the fire of God. I believe the main thing holding this up is the fear of man. Most believers seem to fear man more than they fear God. The real question is: Do you have enough faith to fight with fire? I remind you once more of what the Word of God declares in the book of James. James 5:17-18, *"Elijah was a human being, even as we are. He prayed earnestly that it would not rain, and it did not rain on the land for three and a half years. Again he prayed, and the heavens gave rain, and the earth produced its crops."*

Remember who you are! If you are a person like Elijah, will you be able to fight like Elijah! Will you be able to fight with the fire of God! This raises another question. How should we use fire to fight enemies? Remember it is not your enemies we are talking about. We are talking about the enemies of God. If we had the power of the fire of God without the love of God, we would be very dangerous people. We must always season everything with the love of God. We do not choose the time to fight with fire. On the other hand we need to be ready to do as we are commanded by the Lord. Amen?

Do not take revenge, my friends, but leave room for God's wrath, for it is written: "It is mine to avenge; I will repay," says the Lord. On the contrary: "If your enemy is hungry, feed him; if he is thirsty, give him something to drink. In doing this, you will heap burning coals on his head." Do not be overcome by evil, but overcome evil with good. (Romans 12:19-21, NIV)

Love and kindness are like burning coals when they fall on the enemy and those who follow him. Remember that our weapons are not carnal but powerful in the spiritual realm. I believe the main calling we receive in fighting with fire is to use it against enemy strongholds. In the realm of the spirit, we show no mercy to the forces of evil! As led by the Holy Spirit, we call down the fire of God on them! We don't take any prisoners from the demon armies!

This may sound too violent at first. Many people walk away when I talk about spiritual warfare. They don't want any part of it. There is a false teaching which says that if you do not fight the enemy, he will not fight you. I assure you that this is not the case. The enemy has a plan for your life and you can read what Yeshua ha Messiach said about it in John 10:10, "*The thief does not come except to steal, and to kill, and to destroy. I have come that they may have life, and that they may have it more abundantly.*" It is important to know that the enemy does not stop because you are unaware or unprepared. He has a plan for you which is the opposite of the Lord's plan. Remember who the enemy is. We don't fight against people (Even if we sometimes want to). We are at war with principalities, powers, rulers of darkness and wicked spirits residing in the second heaven.

For our struggle is not against flesh and blood, but against the rulers, against the authorities, against the powers of this dark world and against the spiritual forces of evil in the heavenly realms. (Ephesians 6:12, NIV)

We do not war against flesh and blood! Remember who you are called to be and remember what you are called to do. Even the most faithful disciples can get confused about spiritual warfare. Remember how Jesus had to deal with this in His group of disciples (Luke 9:52-56). Even members of His inner circle got confused. As you study this passage again, think about what the Lord is saying to you about your battles. Think about what He is saying about the use of fire.

We are called to always seek and travel on the high road. We must never stoop to revenge or hatred. We are disciples of the Kingdom of God and we are ambassadors of His love. Love is very powerful. It is more powerful than fire. Remember Proverbs 25:21-22, "*If your enemy is hungry, give him food to eat; if he is thirsty, give him water to drink. In doing this, you will heap burning coals on his head, and the Lord will reward you.*" In truth, love is like fire to demonic spirits. Instead of vengeance because of an offense, we rise above these emotions and accept the higher calling. Think about this:

Bless those who persecute you; bless and do not curse. Rejoice with those who rejoice; mourn with those who mourn. Live in harmony with one another. Do not be proud, but be willing to associate with people of low position. Do not be conceited. Do not repay anyone evil for evil. Be careful to do what is right in the eyes of everyone. If it is possible, as far as it depends on you, live at peace with everyone. Do not take revenge, my dear friends, but leave room for God's wrath, for it is written: "It is mine to avenge; I will repay," says the Lord. On the contrary: "If your enemy is hungry, feed him; if he is thirsty, give him something to drink. In doing this, you will heap burning coals on his head." Do not be overcome by evil, but overcome evil with good." (Romans 12:14-21, NIV)

ENEMY FIRE

In our study of scripture and our experiences of spiritual warfare, we quickly learn that the enemy always counterfeits the things of God. Then he works to tempt people to accept his version of the story. It began in the Garden of Eden, when he tempted the first two people to see the Word of God in a twisted way. It worked and he hasn't changed his tactics over the centuries. Tragically, it is still working.

Part of the enemy's counterfeit spirituality is "unauthorized fire." He managed to deceive the first two sons of Aaron and they were removed because of their rebellion against the Lord. He did it again with the 250 Levites who followed Korah and came before the Lord with unauthorized fire. They didn't learn the lesson from Aaron's sons, and suffered the same outcome. You must always remember that the enemy has fire, but it will never be the kind of fire approved of the Lord.

Then I saw another beast coming up out of the earth, and he had two horns like a lamb *and spoke like a dragon. And he exercises all the authority of the first beast in his presence, and causes the earth and those who dwell in it to worship the first beast, whose deadly wound was healed. He performs great signs, so that he even **makes fire come down from heaven** on the earth in the sight of men. And he deceives those who dwell on the earth by those signs which he was granted to do in the sight of the beast, telling those who dwell on the earth to make an image to the beast who was wounded by the sword and lived.* (Revelation 13:11-14)

The enemy's fire is limited. It is only coming down from the second heaven where everything false and wicked resides. In spite of the limitations, he still deceives those who dwell on the earth. You must seek always to operate in the spiritual gift of "discerning of spirits." (see 1 Corinthians 12:10) You cannot assume that all spiritual fire is from the Lord. The devil also uses his fire in attempting to destroy his enemies. As you remain aware of this enemy fire, you do not get into fear. You have something to protect you. Spiritual armor is available to you. Claim this gift from the Lord and be certain to wear your armor at all times. Do this as you read Ephesians 6:16 (NIV), "*In addition to all this, take up the shield of faith, with which you can extinguish all the flaming arrows of the evil one.*"

For the weapons of our warfare are not carnal but mighty in God for pulling down strongholds, casting down arguments and every high thing that exalts itself against the knowledge of God, bringing every thought into captivity to the obedience of Christ, and being ready to punish all disobedience when your obedience is fulfilled. (2 Corinthians 10:4-6)

Flaming arrows can be harmful, but you need not fear them. You have the mighty *"shield of faith."* Use it wisely. It is powerful. Remember that your spiritual weapons are *"mighty in God."* With the shield of faith, you do more than merely block the flaming arrows of the enemy. You extinguish them. It is all about faith. Faith is very powerful. You can always extinguish enemy fire with the power of your faith! Remember how to build up this faith: Romans 10:17, *"So then faith comes by hearing, and hearing by the word of God."* I am repeating this for a reason. I want you to begin to repeat these powerful promises of the Lord until they become a major part of you strong and growing faith.

Faith is a little like fire. When you use your faith against enemy fire, you are fighting fire with fire. Remember that the enemy's fire is limited, but the fire of God is unlimited. It is powerful and will always triumph in the end. So begin now to fight God's way. Fight with the fire of God which has come to you. God has anointed you with fire as a living sacrifice. Use it wisely.

HOW TO REKINDLE A FIRE

What can you do if the fire of God goes out in your life and ministry? Like the children of Israel, we are cautioned to keep the fire burning night and day. But what if it goes out. Is there anything we can do? The truth is that there is nothing that we can do, but that is not the end of the story. With God all things are possible. I want you to think about this question as your remember what Jesus said in Luke 12:49, *"I came to send fire on the earth, and how I wish it were already kindled!*" I believe that one of the ways to understand this word from the Lord is to see it as follows: Jesus came to restart the fire of God in His people.

Many People are like wet wood. If you have ever been on a camping trip, you probably learned many lessons. One thing most campers learn is that it is not easy to start a fire when the wood is wet. At times we need a miracle like Elijah experienced. The fire of God set the wet wood ablaze. The fire of God consumed the entire sacrifice in an instant. It even consumed the stones and the water in the trench. The Lord knows how to start a fire. Remember how the Lord set the disciples on fire.

> *When the Day of Pentecost had fully come, they were all with one accord in one place. And suddenly there came a sound from heaven, as of a rushing mighty wind, and it filled the whole house where they were sitting. Then there appeared to them divided tongues, as of fire, and one sat upon each of them. And they were all filled with the Holy Spirit and began to speak with other tongues, as the Spirit gave them utterance.* (Acts 2:1-4)

He did it by baptizing them with the Holy Spirit and fire. To make this work clear, the flames divided and came down on each of the one hundred and twenty people gathered in the Upper Room. No one was left out. No one remained cold that day. The fire brought something wonderful with it. The fire imparted spiritual power to these early evangelists. The fire imparted the authority of the Lord. They went into the streets and began to set Jerusalem on fire.

From there it spread around the world and now it is available to you wherever you are today.

Unfortunately, we still see so many in the church who seem to have lost the fire. Many seem to have grown cold in our day and time. So, what happened to that fire of God? Where is the fire in modern day disciples? Where is the power and the authority today? The fires have gone out in many denominations, churches and believers. This is tragic and we may not like to hear it, but it is the truth. Is there any hope left for those who have lost the fire of God? Absolutely! But, how do we get God's fire power back into the Body of Christ?

> *Furthermore the word of the Lord came to me, saying, "Son of man, set your face toward the south; preach against the south and prophesy against the forest land, the South, and say to the forest of the South, 'Hear the word of the Lord!'" Thus says the Lord GOD: "Behold, I will kindle a fire in you, and it shall devour every green tree and every dry tree in you; the blazing flame shall not be quenched, and all faces from the south to the north shall be scorched by it. All flesh shall see that I, the Lord, have kindled it; it shall not be quenched."* (Ezekiel 20:45-47)

ASKING GOD TO SEND FIRE

It's time to ask the Lord to send fire on his people once again! Have you noticed that most of the instances of God's fire being released came as a response to the prayers of the faithful believers? It's time for the faithful to get on their knees again, and cry out for more fire. It is time for the faithful to get on their faces and proclaim once again in faith that the Lord is good and His mercy endures forever. In former times, it was considered a great honor to carry God's fire. Are you ready and willing to be honored by carrying the fire of God once more to a new generation?

PRAYER

Deal bountifully with Your servant, so I can live and keep Your word. Open my eyes so I may behold wondrous things from Your Torah (Teaching). I am a stranger in the earth. Do not hide Your commandments from me. My inner being breaks for the longing for Your judgments at all times. You have rebuked the proud who are cursed, who go astray from Your commandments. Remove reproach and contempt from me; for I have kept Your testimonies. Princes also sat, speaking against me, but Your servant did meditate in Your statutes. Your testimonies also are my delight and my counselors. (Psalm 119:17-24, ONMB)

PAUSE AND REFLECT

1. Name three ways the Lord uses fire in His work on Earth.

2. What can you do to help release the fire of revival?

3. In what ways has the Lord shown approval of your prayers with His fire?

4. How can you pray for the fire of God to come to you?

5. What kind of fire does the enemy use and how can you deal with it?

6. What can you do if the fire of God goes out in your life and ministry?

CHAPTER TWELVE

FIRE IS TRANSFERABLE

J ust after 7:00 p.m. during one of the revival services at Morningstar Fellowship Church in Fort Mill, South Carolina, I was carried to Heaven for an extended visit. This was the revival carried back to Morningstar Fellowship Church from the Lakeland Revival by some teenagers in 2008. We had spent twelve days in the Lakeland Revival and believed the prophecy of it spreading to other areas. When it broke out at Morningstar, we journeyed there from our home in Texas in order to keep the revival fires going in our own lives. I believe that it was that hunger which opened Heaven for me that day. The experience I was given in Heaven with the Lord was an awesome encounter for me and I am still highly influenced by what the Lord did for me during our time together. Below you can read my report of that visit. I pray that as you read it the Lord will do something similar for you.

Vision Report, September 17, 2008,
Vision of Unfinished Heaven:

In the Fall of 2008, we attended the Harvest Fest Conference at Morningstar Fellowship Church in Fort Mill,

SC. During one of the worship services as very loud music was being released by the worship team, I was lifted up to Heaven for an extended visit and experienced a life changing encounter with the Lord. What I experienced in that visit to Heaven gave me an entirely new outlook on ministry and the teachings of the Bible about the second coming of Jesus. That day I was sitting very straight in the chair because this is a very comfortable position for an experience like the one I was given. I had my hands palms down on top of my legs when the Spirit lifted me up to an open portal into Heaven.

As I looked up through the open portal, something like dark clouds repeatedly moved across to block my view into Heaven. I knew this was a move by the enemy to prevent me from having this experience. I repeated the words of James 4:7, "*Therefore submit to God. Resist the devil and he will flee from you.*" After I spoke this verse, the clouds dispersed and I was able to see through the portal again. After a very short period of time, the clouds came back to block my view. This happened several times and I began to realize that the enemy is very persistent in his attempts to block us from receiving what the Lord has for us. So, I pressed in until I moved past the clouds. I was then in the middle of the portal with my head and shoulder above it and my feet below it.

At this point, I saw a small red light moving overhead from my right to the left. It seemed very high above me and I watched it slowly moving overhead. Then the Lord asked, "Do you want that?" I wasn't sure what it was, but felt confident in asking for it since the Lord was releasing it in Heaven. I said, "Yes!" Then the Lord motioned with His eyes toward my left hand which was palm down on my left leg. At this point, I was very detached in my spirit from my body. I was aware that my body was still in the worship center, but it seemed very far away. From the motion by Jesus, I knew that I had to turn my hand over in the natural and lift it upward to receive what the Lord was releasing in the spiritual realm. That proved to be very difficult because of my detachment from the body. It seemed like I was moving a ton of weight in that hand. It took a long time for me to finally achieve the goal of turning my palm upward in readiness to receive what the Lord was giving.

The little red light moved toward my hand and I could finally see exactly what it was. As it got closer, it looked larger. When it came into my hand, I could see that it was a very large ruby about the size of an egg. I was delighted to receive it and to see it in my hand. It was so real to my eyes and my touch that I expected to still have it when the experience in Heaven was over. I asked the Lord, "What is it?" He replied, "It is the love of the Father coming to you as a gift for your ministry." As I watched the ruby, it began to merge or melt into the palm of my hand. Then I knew this was a spiritual manifestation rather than something I would have in the natural. As it continued to merge with my left hand, I asked the Lord, "Shouldn't this be in my right hand so that I can impart it to others?" The Lord responded, "When you stand face to face and impart it to others, you will place it in their right (correct) hand. Remember that your heart is on your left side and this is the correct place for you to carry this gift from the Father." The Ruby continued to melt into my hand and I suddenly felt extreme heat in that hand. It began to burn intensely. The pain continued to grow, but I didn't want it to stop. I wanted more.

As I mentally tried to process what I had received, I saw something moving above toward my right hand. The Lord asked, "Do you want that one too?" As I looked at this one, I saw that it was a dull colored black looking stone. It was not shining, and I wasn't really sure if I wanted this one. However, the Lord was offering it and I decided that I should take it. Then the Lord gestured toward my right hand which was still face down on my leg, and said, "Well?" Again, I had great difficulty turning my hand over and raising it up to receive this gift from the Lord. I learned from this experience to always have my hands open and uplifted when I go into His presence.

As this object came close to my hand, I could see it more clearly. I was very surprised to see that it was a lump of coal. In many old American Christmas stories and songs, the naughty children receive a lump of coal in their stockings from Santa Claus. I hoped that there was a different meaning for this stone. I asked the Lord to tell me what it meant, and He said, "It is a diamond in the rough. As you minister in the Kingdom, it will continuously be polished and eventually be clearly seen as a diamond of great value." This really sounded good. So, I welcomed this gift from the Lord. However, I was surprised when it landed in the palm of my hand. It began to burn like fire in my hand, and I felt the burning and the roughness of the stone wearing against my skin.

The burning in both of my hands was constant day and night for more than two years. The pain from the fire of the Lord was sometimes almost unbearable. At times, I would place my hands under cold running water to cool them down, but as soon as I pulled my hands from the water, the burning would almost instantly come back to full intensity. My wife experienced this same thing. This reassured me of something I understood from the Lord. Everything I receive in these Third Heaven visits is also available to others who hear about them or read about them. They are available to all who are willing to receive what the Lord is releasing. The fire still comes and goes in my hands and in my wife's hands after all this time. This almost always accompanies our ministry in the anointing. We have also seen many people receive the fire after hearing the testimony. Remember Revelation 19:10b, *"For the testimony of Jesus is the spirit of prophecy."*

After receiving both stones, the Lord lifted me up through the portal into Heaven. Together we flew about fifty feet in the air over many miles of the landscape of Heaven. My goal was to see the Holy City. This was such a powerful longing in my heart, but it would not be met during this visit. I traveled with the Lord over miles and miles of rolling hills with beautiful valleys surrounding them on all sides. There was a roadway between the mountains with crossroads in every valley. However there were no people anywhere in all the miles we travelled. I asked the Lord to help me understand. At first, I did not receive a response. We just continued to travel for a very long distance. Finally, we came to a beautiful river lined with trees on both sides. I knew what this was. It was the river of living water, and it was so exciting for me to see it. You probably knew what it was as you read my description.

> *"Then the angel showed me the river of the water of life, as clear as crystal, flowing from the throne of God and of the Lamb down the middle of the great street of the city. On each side of the river stood the tree of life, bearing twelve crops of fruit, yielding its fruit every month. And the leaves of the tree are for the healing of the nations."* (Revelation 22:1-2, NIV)

We continued to fly along the path of the river for many miles as it took a winding route through the countryside. In all the miles we traveled, I did not see one single person on the ground or near the river. It was beautiful and I wanted to go down and soak in the water, but that also had to wait for another visit. I asked the Lord once again to help me understand the meaning of this experience. Finally, He revealed it to me and I received it with mixed emotions. I was very happy to get an understanding of what all of this meant, but the answer caused a very deep pain in my spirit. The Lord said, "This is the unoccupied part of Heaven. It should be filled with people, but my church has not done its job. The people who were to live here have never been reached by the Gospel of the Kingdom. They were never given a chance to accept it and come to their heavenly home!"

When I heard that, I began to weep bitterly. Then I knew why I had received those two stones and I knew why I felt so much pain from carrying them. I had to have that love of God in my heart to realize how much pain the Lord felt because of lost souls. I knew His pain in my limited capacity and the hurt was almost overwhelming. I wondered about the pain He was carrying in His heart and marveled at His capacity to carry such a heavy weight. I felt a great sense of responsibility for part of these empty spaces. A great desire to win the lost rose up from deep within my heart. This almost unbearable heartache for the lost continues to this very day. That is why I said that this was a life changing experience for me. The fire in my hands was so intense that I could not forget this Word from the Lord for even a few minutes. I continue to feel the pain and my desire to win the lost continues to this day. I pray that you will receive this intense fire, pain and desire from the Lord as you read the messages in this book.

As I wiped the tears from my eyes, I saw a great light in the distance. My first thought was that it was the light coming from the Holy City. I was either being moved toward this glorious light or it was moving toward me. I didn't really know which because my eyes were so filled with tears. I didn't notice at this point that I was now accompanied by an angel rather than the Lord. My excitement began to build at the possibility of seeing the Holy City. The pain I was feeling in my heart was being slightly replaced by joy and excitement at what I was about to see. When the amazing light of His glory got closer I was able to see that this was coming from the Lord Jesus and a great company of the white robed army of the Lord. The light of His glory was so strong that I could hardly see details because I had to keep my eyes almost closed in the brightness of His radiance.

When the Lord got very close, I heard Him speak with great power and great authority, "I am coming very soon, and my people are not ready!" Wow! That pronouncement was painful to hear. All I could think about was how to warn the people to get ready for His return. I felt almost powerless to deal with this information. What could I do to let people know what the Lord said? Then He spoke again in almost the same words, "Behold! I am coming very soon, and my church is not prepared!"

(End of Vision Report)
IMPORTANCE OF BEING ON FIRE

In this season of the Spirit, it is very important for every believer to be on fire and fired up for the great harvest before us. I can still hear the words and feel the sadness of the Lord when He first spoke to me, "I am coming very soon, and my people are not ready!" I don't want to grow cold in these closing hours of our time on Earth. I continue to pray often for more fire. The Lord gave me an intense reminder. For over two years my hands burned from that fire twenty four hours a day, seven days a week. It still returns often as a constant reminder of the call of the Lord.

After returning from this experience in Heaven, I shared this with my wife. As I shared this vision report her hands began to burn as well. Two important lessons were revealed in this experience. First, I learned from firsthand experience that I could feel the heat emanating from her hands as she had said she could feel from mine. From this experience I became even more intensely aware of the reality of this fire from the Lord which now resided in both of us. The second and possibly more important lesson was that the fire is transferable. It had been trans-ferred to her just through my giving an account of my experience. I related this once again to the teaching in Revelation 19:10, *"For the testimony of Jesus is the spirit of prophecy."*

As we shared this experience in other churches and with other people, they also began to feel the fire. In one church I noticed the pastor behaving in an unusual manner as I spoke. He left the front of the church and began to walk up and down the aisles. At some point, he would turn and go back in order to walk forward in another aisle. After the service, he explained that he had felt a great amount of heat radiating from my presence as I was speaking. He had gone out into the congregation to see how far away he could feel that heat. He was feeling it past the worship area in front of the pews and then four rows deep into the seating. The heat from the fire was tangible and strong. This was a new learning for us about how the Lord can touch others with His fire which He placed in us. He can do the same for you and through you as you minister.

As I shared this experience in other settings, I began to notice a phenomena which occurred over and over. As I shared the story, many people would lean forward in their pews because it was such a new idea for them. Those who leaned forward more than others reported that they suddenly felt the same fire in their hands. I could tell exactly when it happened because of their behavior. They would suddenly seem to freeze in place and then look down into the palms of their hands. Then they would look up at me again and then back into their hands. For these people there was no need for a special time of impartation after the message. Like my wife they were receiving it through the testimony of what Jesus had done for me.

FIRE IS TRANSFERABLE

For God is my witness, whom I serve with my spirit in the gospel of His Son, that without ceasing I make mention of you always in my prayers, making request if, by some means, now at last I may find a way in the will of God to come to you. For I long to see you, that I may impart to you some spiritual gift, so that you may be established—that is, that I may be encouraged together with you by the mutual faith both of you and me. (Romans 1:9-12)

Like Paul, I am always desiring to impart spiritual gifts to others. This is one of my regular prayers when I am in His presence. I believe this is the attitude we should all have about the gifts of the Spirit we have received. Nothing was meant for private use. In 1 Corinthians 12:7, we are reminded, *"But the manifestation of the Spirit is given to each one for the profit of all:"* Every spiritual gift and every blessing is given for a purpose. All these are given to build up the body of Christ and every member of the body. Read again the teaching of Paul in Ephesians 4:12, "...*for the equipping of the saints for the work of ministry, for the edifying of the body of Christ...*" This is God's purpose in releasing spiritual gifts to you and me.

Impartation has always been an important part of our relationship with the Lord. Moses took the leaders up on the mountain so that the Lord could take some of the Spirit which was on him and put it on the other leaders. Moses was not diminished in this process and his spiritual gifts were not lessened. The Lord had also taught this lesson to Abraham. His blessings increased as he passed them on to others. Genesis 12:2-3, "*I will make you a great nation; I will bless you and make your name great; and you shall be a blessing. I will bless those who bless you, and I will curse him who curses you; and in you all the families of the earth shall be blessed.*" You will never be in danger of giving away too much in the Spirit. The more you give the more you have. In time, Abraham's blessing extended to the whole world.

> *And the people asked him, saying, what shall we do then? He answereth and saith unto them, He that hath two coats, let him impart to him that hath none; and he that hath meat, let him do likewise.* (Luke 3:10-11, KJV)

Just as we can bless others by imparting things to them in the natural, we can bless them by providing the things they need in their spirits. We can release a warm spiritual covering for those whose fires have grown cold. We can reach out to others and give them life giving and life-saving support. The Lord has released so much to us as believers, and He calls us to pass it on. If you are called to be a fire carrier, then you are likely called to be a Holy Spirit fire starter.

> *Let no corrupt word proceed out of your mouth, but what is good for necessary edification, that it may impart grace to the hearers. And do not grieve the Holy Spirit of God, by whom you were sealed for the day of redemption.* (Ephesians 4:29-30)

Think about what the passage above is saying. It grieves the Holy Spirit when people use their gifts for the flesh rather than for the Spirit. We were given the gift of speech so that we could impart grace to those who hear our words. We must be very careful in the use of this gift. Every gift which begins for good can be corrupted and used by the enemy for evil. We must not let that happen. Consider the words of Proverbs 27:17, "*As iron sharpens iron, so a man sharpens the countenance of his friend.*" The big question is: Are we helping to sharpen one another? This is an important part of our calling and we must not ignore these gifts of the Holy Spirit. We must not hide His fire.

> *So, affectionately longing for you, we were well pleased to impart to you not only the gospel of God, but also our own lives, because you had become dear to us.* (1 Thessalonians 2:8)

Think about your ministry. Are you intentionally imparting your spiritual gifts to others? When we have this spirit in us we do more than just pass along gifts.

We are actually imparting our own lives. If Paul was well pleased to impart to the Thessalonians, think about how good you will feel knowing that you have given of yourself to so many others. This is the richness of our relationships and the hope of His glory.

If you can accept what I have shared in this chapter, I want to take it another step. I want to impart this fire to you. There are several ways to do this. I have included prayers at the end of each chapter in hopes that you will receive an impartation of the fire of the Holy Spirit. Now, it is time to go one more step. I want you to receive that impartation the way so many others have. Read the vision report again from the beginning of this chapter. As you read it, lean into it. Extend your hands in front of you in a position to receive. Press into this gift and let more of the Holy Spirit fire fall on you.

During an extended ministry trip I was sharing this impartation in one meeting after another. During this time, my hands were on fire and the pain was intense. Once again, the only relief I could get was to place my hands under running water. As soon as I removed my hands from the cool water, the fire returned. During this time I prayed over and over, "More fire Lord! More Fire! It hurts so good!" One night, I woke up at about 3:00 a.m. I was sitting up in bed with my hands extended in front of me. They were on fire and the pain was intense. Yet, I heard myself praying in my sleep, "More fire Lord! More Fire! It hurts so good!"

That night, I realized that I was praying for fire in my sleep. I had focused so much on my desire for more fire that it even manifested when I slept. I want to impart that to you also. I believe it came from my repetition of that prayer during my waking hours. It began to build in my spirit first and then in my mind. It became an automatic response to cry out for more fire. When you desire it that much, the Lord responds. When you want more of Him and a closer walk with Him, He responds. When you want it so much that you cry out day and night, fire will come. Amen?

PRAYER

Deal bountifully with Your servant, so I can live and keep Your word. Open my eyes so I may behold wondrous things from Your Torah (Teaching). I am a stranger in the earth. Do not hide Your commandments from me. My inner being breaks for the longing for Your judgments at all times. You have rebuked the proud who are cursed, who go astray from Your commandments. Remove reproach and contempt from me; for I have kept Your testimonies. Princes also sat, speaking against me, but Your servant did meditate in Your statutes. Your testimonies also are my delight and my counselors. (Psalm 119:17-24, ONMB)

PAUSE AND REFLECT

1. Describe one of your spiritual gifts and how it was imparted to you.

2. Have you experienced the impartation of fire? If so, describe it below.

3. What do you believe about the impartation of Holy Spirit fire?

4. Do you still want the gift of fire knowing that it can burn?

5. What kind of plan do you have to seek more fire?

6. If you felt fire as you read the testimony again, describe what happened.

SUMMARY

A FIRE FALLS
SERIOUS CHOICES NEED TO BE MADE

As I was writing this summary, the Lord reminded me that there are serious choices we need to make. This has always been true. Each generation is called to make choices about whether they will serve the Lord or not. They are also called to make a decision about carrying the fire of God. Now these questions come down to you and me. Are we ready for the return of our Lord? Will we be confident of our service when we stand before His judgment seat?

> *So we are always confident, knowing that while we are at home in the body we are absent from the Lord. For we walk by faith, not by sight. We are confident, yes, well pleased rather to be absent from the body and to be present with the Lord. Therefore we make it our aim, whether present or absent, to be well pleasing to Him. For we must all appear before the judgment seat of Christ, that each one may receive the things done in the body, according to what he has*

done, whether good or bad. Knowing, there-
fore, the terror of the Lord, we persuade men;
but we are well known to God, and I also
trust are well known in your consciences. (2
Corinthians 5:6-11)

The Lord does not want us to be fearful. He wants us to be confident of where we stand in our relationship with Him. He has given us guidelines and helps throughout the Scriptures to provide what we need. He has manifested His power, His presence and His fire in our lives and the lives of others so that through our shared testimonies we can build each other up. As we share what the Lord has done it provides strength and comfort to other believers and unbelievers alike. I pray that you and I will be as well known to the Lord as Paul was. I pray that our faith and our service will always be pleasing to Him. Amen?

I pray that the words of my testimonies in this book will encourage you to go on an adventure of discovery for yourself. I pray that you will receive more revelation in your search than I did in mine as I prepared to write this down for you. We must always be seeking more of Him and a greater revelation in the Spirit. I pray that a fresh anointing of the Spirit of wisdom and revelation will be released to you so that you may increase more and more in your faith and in the strength of His holy fire. I pray that the Spirit of truth will be a constant guide for you and lead you as Jesus promised into all the truth you need in your relationship with the Lord and your service in the kingdom of God.

For we shall all stand before the judgment
seat of Christ. For it is written: "As I live, says
the LORD, every knee shall bow to Me, and

every tongue shall confess to God." So then each of us shall give account of himself to God. Therefore let us not judge one another anymore, but rather resolve this, not to put a stumbling block or a cause to fall in our brother's way. (Romans 14:10b-13)

It is not our task to judge the relationship and service of others to our Lord. It is our task to examine ourselves to see if we are in that right relationship with Him. It is far better to do this today than to face Him unprepared. Look back over the questions at the end of each chapter. These questions were written to help you answer for yourself about your service to the Lord. We are being called to carry the fire of God and to be fire starters in the great end time harvest. I pray that we are ready. Amen?

PRAYER

Now may our Lord Jesus Christ Himself, and our God and Father, who has loved us and given us everlasting consolation and good hope by grace, comfort your hearts and establish you in every good word and work. (2 Thessalonians 2:16-17)

Now to the King eternal, immortal, invisible, to God who alone is wise, be honor and glory forever and ever. Amen. (1 Timothy 1:17)

APPENDIX ONE

OILS OF THE WORD

Now it may seem strange to you for me to add an appendix about the various oils mentioned in the Bible at the end of a book on the fire of the Lord. That is okay. It was strange to me as well. I kept feeling a stronger and stronger call to put this in the book for some of you. There is some special connection between the oils and the fire which is yet to be fully revealed. So, I am doing it by faith and praying that the revelation will come to both you and me. Amen?

Over and over during the past few months, the Lord has touched my spirit to do research on the various types and uses of oil in the Scriptures. The things referenced below emerged from that research. As we minister in the fire of the Lord, we will need many of the oils of anointing as well as the oils of healing when we are burned. We will need the holy oils released in the ministry of Yeshua ha Messiach to prepare us to be able to move into the flames of His glory and survive. May you be blessed by these added messages!

The order of presentation was not planned. I simply added these as I discovered them. I am trusting the Lord to bring order to these lessons from His Word. I believe

He will do this. For example, the first oil which appeared in my research was for healing. I believe that many people who read this are in need of healing. As they are anointed by the Lord and by the elders, their healing may be a confirmation of what the Lord is doing in their lives to prepare them for the future. As a result of these thoughts it seemed appropriate for this oil to come first in this section.

OIL FOR HEALING

*Take thou also unto thee principal spices, of pure myrrh five hundred shekels, and of sweet cinnamon half so much, even two hundred and fifty shekels, and of sweet calamus two hundred and fifty shekels, And of cassia five hundred shekels, after the shekel of the sanctuary, and of oil olive an hin: And thou shalt make it an **oil of holy ointment**, an ointment compound after the **art of the apothecary**: it shall be an holy anointing oil.* (Exodus 30:23-25, KJV)

So they went out and preached that people should repent. And they cast out many demons, and anointed with oil many who were sick, and healed them. (Mark 6:12-13)

Is anyone among you sick? Let him call for the elders of the church, and let them pray over him, anointing him with oil in the name of the Lord. And the prayer of faith will save the sick, and the Lord will raise him up. And if he has committed sins, he will be forgiven. (James 5:14-15)

OIL OF ANOINTING

*You shall not go out from the door of the tabernacle of meeting, lest you die, for the **anointing oil** of the LORD is upon you. And they did according to the word of Moses."* (Leviticus 10:7)

This is a reference to the oil used in the ordination service of the priests. It is very holy and cannot be carried out from the presence of the Lord. I believe this speaks to another revelation found in 1 Timothy 5:22, *"Do not lay hands on anyone hastily, nor share in other people's sins; keep yourself pure."* It is easy for us to become too hasty in sharing the holy things of the Lord with others. This is a reminder that it is His work and we need to be obedient to Him in order to please Him. We do not mix the holy with the profane without risking a rebuke from the Lord. We must listen carefully to all the instruction we receive from the Spirit of truth.

*He must not enter a place where there is a dead body. He must not make himself unclean, even for his father or mother, nor leave the sanctuary of his God or desecrate it, because he has been **dedicated** by the **anointing oil** of his God. I am the LORD.* (Leviticus 21:11-12, NIV)

I have found My servant David; with My holy oil I have anointed him, (Psalm 89:20)

OIL OF PREPARATION FOR SERVICE

*Each young woman's turn came to go in to King Ahasuerus after she had completed twelve months' **preparation**, according to the regulations for the women, for thus were the days of their preparation apportioned: six months with **oil of myrrh**, and six months with perfumes and preparations for beautifying women.* (Esther 2:12)

We have often spoken of myrrh in relationship to the burial of the dead. One aspect of preparation is what was done with the dead, but it seems that the Lord has a meaning beyond this. Esther was prepared by soaking in the oil of myrrh for six months. There is a kind of oil which prepares us to be in the presence of the King of kings and Lord of lords. He provides the oil and only asks us to spend time soaking in it before rushing into the Secret Place unprepared. Remember the promise given by the previous generation of missionaries: "Where the Lord doth guide, the Lord doth provide."

OIL OF GLADNESS

*You love righteousness and hate wickedness; therefore God, Your God, has anointed You with the **oil of gladness** more than Your companions. All Your garments are scented with myrrh and aloes and cassia, out of the ivory palaces, by which they have made You glad.* (Psalm 45:7-8)

The oil of gladness is administered directly by the Lord. This anointing comes to those who are righteous in His eyes. A further condition is that it is reserved to bless those who hate wickedness. From this passage it seems that there are degrees of the release of this oil. The more your life is characterize as being in right relationship with the Lord the more of this oil is poured out. I believe the term "gladness" is multi-dimensional. It makes the Lord glad when His people love righteousness and hate wickedness. Then this outpouring of oil blesses them with this same gladness. A large part of that gladness is the knowledge that your life and work are pleasing to the Lord.

OIL OF JOY

To console those who mourn in Zion, to give them beauty for ashes, the **oil of joy** *for mourning, the garment of praise for the spirit of heaviness; that they may be called trees of righteousness, the planting of the* LORD, *that He may be glorified.* (Isaiah 61:3)

There are at least two powerful companion verses which go with this oil. The first is Psalm 30:5, "*For His anger is but for a moment, His favor is for life; weeping may endure for a night, but joy comes in the morning.*" And then there is Nehemiah 8:10b (NIV), "*Do not grieve, for the joy of the Lord is your strength.*" Joy brings great power to overcome the painful things in life. It is the source of great spiritual strength and is an excellent companion to all those who serve the Lord. May the oil of joy never cease to flow in our lives!

OIL OF SPIKENARD
(For the bride of Christ)

And being in Bethany at the house of Simon the leper, as He sat at the table, a woman came having an alabaster flask of very costly __oil of spikenard__. Then she broke the flask and poured it on His head. (Mark 14:3)

There are at least two primary functions for the Oil of Spikenard. The most prominent and well recognized use comes from the anointing of Jesus for His burial. It is also closely associated with the bride because of the prominence in Song of Songs 1:12, *"While the king is at his table, my spikenard sends forth its fragrance.* Along with Song of Songs 4:13-14, this oil is closely associated with the fragrance of the bride of Christ. It is this fragrance which should cover us as we sit in the presence of the King of kings.

OIL OF OFFERING

Thus they shall prepare the lamb, the grain offering, and the oil, as a regular burnt offering every morning. (Ezekiel 46:15)

Oil was included in the description of many of the sacrificial offering prepared in the Tabernacle and Temple. Oil seems to make the sacrifices burn with a sweeter fragrance. As living sacrifices, we too need to offer ourselves as a sweet fragrance to the Lord, and this oil reminds us of this idea. Oil is not only offered to the Lord, but it is an offering given back by Him to His faithful people. We see this in Ezekiel 16:19, *"Also My food which I gave you—the pastry of fine flour, oil, and honey which I fed you—you set it before them as sweet incense; and so it was," says the Lord GOD.*

This is a powerful reminder of the need for our relationship with the Lord and every relationship to be characterized by a two-way exchange of gifts. Oil is also a gift from the Lord for the preparation of our food. As such it is another offering from Him to make our lives more pleasant and satisfying. Ezekiel 16:13, "*Thus you were adorned with gold and silver, and your clothing was of fine linen, silk, and embroidered cloth. You ate pastry of fine flour, honey, and oil.*"

OIL OF SATISFACTION

The LORD will answer and say to His people, "Behold, I will send you grain and new wine and oil, and you will be satisfied by them; I will no longer make you a reproach among the nations." (Joel 2:19)

Oil is a gift from the Lord to bring a sense of satisfaction to His people. The many and varied uses of oil point to the fullness of this gift from the Lord. It is also given as a sign to others of the Lord's favor on your life and work. This kind of oil is one of the powerful testimonies of Jesus which is also filled with the Spirit of prophecy. When the oil begins to flow in your ministry, others can clearly see that the blessing and favor of the Lord is present in your work. This gives us a wonderful sense of satisfaction because all of our work is producing fruit fit for the kingdom of God.

GOLDEN OIL OF WITNESS

*Then I answered and said to him, "What are these two olive trees—at the right of the lampstand and at its left?" And I further answered and said to him, "What are these two olive branches that drip into the receptacles of the two gold pipes from which the **golden oil** drains?"* (Zechariah 4:11-12)

The golden oil represents pure and holy service to the Lord. The two who stand beside the Lord are making offerings which are so pure that the glory of God manifests in the flow of oil. For a full explanation of who these are, you have to go to Revelation 11:3-4 (NIV), *"And I will give power to my two witnesses, and they will prophesy for 1,260 days, clothed in sackcloth." These are the two olive trees and the two lampstands that stand before the Lord of the earth."* This is about the two faithful witnesses who will manifest in the mid part of the tribulation and give a powerful testimony to the truth of the Lord. Their witness flows like golden oil. Perhaps you are called to offer some of this oil to the Lord as well. May the golden oil of a truthful witness never cease to flow!

OIL OF THE LORD'S ANSWER

"It shall come to pass in that day that I will answer," says the LORD; "I will answer the heavens, and they shall answer the earth. The earth shall answer with grain, with new wine, and with oil; they shall answer Jezreel. (Hosea 2:21-22)

This oil when viewed as the Lord's method of answering presents an interesting pattern. According to this verse, the Lord provides the first answer. This answer is to the heavens. Then the heavens give an answer to the earth. And the earth responds (answers back) by producing the things which we need. This entire process speaks of the giving of rain in season which will produce all we need and allow us to respond back with oil. This is a promise for the former rains and the latter rains to come in season. It is given by the Lord for our benefit and to provide something special for us to give back to Him. The Lord's way of doing things is always amazing and wonderful. Amen?

OIL OF PROVISION

Now it came to pass, when the vessels were full, that she said to her son, "Bring me another vessel." And he said to her, "There is not another vessel." So the oil ceased. Then she came and told the man of God. And he said, "Go, sell the oil and pay your debt; and you and your sons live on the rest." (2 Kings 4:6-7)

In a time of great famine when the Lord sent Elisha to the house of a widow and her son who were in great need. The Lord provided for all her needs to get her through the times of lack by letting oil continue to flow until all her vessels and all the containers she could borrow were filled. This speaks to us of the abundance of the Lord's provision. He doesn't offer a small amount. He offers all we can contain. It is the same imagery used in Malachi 3:10b (NIV), *"Test me in this," says the LORD Almighty, "and see if I will not throw open the floodgates of heaven and pour out so much blessing that you will not have room enough for it."* The oil of provision reminds us of the generosity of our Father God who gives until it overflows.

APPENDIX TWO

END TIME HARVEST

VISION REPORT
The Role of Korea and Israel for
The End-time Harvest

In mid-August, as I prayed for our spiritual daughter in Korea, I was given a vision in which I saw a large number "8" hovering over her church. This huge sign looked like a blazing fire of radiant amber color hovering over the church as a proclamation of new beginnings. Think about it. The number eight consists of the number seven (the number of completeness of one era) plus one which points to a new thing following that which has been completed.

The number eight is a powerful prophetic number which appears in many different ways throughout Scriptures. When Noah's Ark was lifted up on the flood waters, there were eight human beings aboard. They were all being called to be a part of God's plan to bring about a new era in human history. Can you imagine beginning the earth all over again with a population of only eight people? Remember that He did it the first time beginning with only one.

In his lengthy relationship with the Lord, Abraham received eight covenant blessings from the Lord. These eight covenant statements covered everything necessary to begin a new nation of people dedicated to the Lord alone. In addition, the Lord establish a new kingdom of priests for the world. Eight always speaks of a powerful new beginning in our lives and in the Lord's destiny for His people on the earth. I love the number eight because it brings so much revelation and provision from the Lord.

There is another very interesting use of the number eight. God commanded that the rite of circumcision was always to be done on the eighth day. This was not an arbitrary number. Each new human being carries the potential of every person who has lived on this planet. Performing this rite on the eighth day symbolized a fresh new start with a fresh new life. Each of these beginnings first starts with a fresh new dedication of some person or persons to the Lord. Are you ready to be dedicated for a fresh new beginning in the Lord?

The next morning, I was given another vision about South Korea. In the vision, I was high in the air over the Korean peninsula. I was looking down as if from something like a satellite view. In this vision, I was shown again the great spiritual warfare occurring in the body of the church. As I agonized over these needless conflicts I saw the number eight again. This time it was over the entire nation and I heard a great proclamation of a new era for the Body of Christ.

The Lord said that this was the third great era in the Korean church. The first era was the great move of Evangelism which built up the church to the level of critical mass. When this mass was achieved, it initiated the second great era. This second era was the era in which many people began to move in the power and the gifts of the Holy Spirit. This era was also characterized by the gifts released by the Spirit of prophecy. As the prophetic move rose in influence, the third great era began to emerge. This will be the release of the great end time harvest.

As with the previous changes in the era of the Spirit, this change was also being met with great resistance by various parts of the church. All the resistance is originating from the enemy. He is finding people within the church who have emotional weaknesses and character defects to rise up in rebellion and block the moves of God. The enemy is fighting ferociously because the new era signals the end of his reign on earth. The enemy's great desire is to delay this era and prolong his time of dominion.

The Lord revealed to me the tactic the enemy is using to accomplish this goal. He wants to distract the church from its destiny and purpose by getting people to look at themselves and to seek their own will and purposes. This will produce a great deal of distraction through jealousy, false accusations, spiritual attacks on one another and an ever growing rebellion. This will be especially strong in those who are under the influence of a Jezebel spirit. In His letter to the church at Thyatira, Jesus warned the church about this time of enemy resistance. He clearly pointed out that it would be released through the workings of the Jezebel spirit. As stated earlier, all seven of these churches represent the church age in which we currently live.

> *Nevertheless I have a few things against, because you allow that woman Jezebel, who calls herself a prophetess, to teach and seduce My servants to commit sexual immorality and eat things sacrificed to idols. And I gave her time to repent of her*

sexual immorality, and she did not repent.
(Revelation 2:20-21)

The Lord will not bless and favor a church which tolerates a Jezebel spirit. This spirit must be cast out by the church. It is important to remember that we are not talking about casting people out of the church. We are talking about casting out the wicked spirit of Jezebel which is bringing sickness, death, and failure to the body of Christ. If those manifesting this spirit do not repent they must leave the church, but we welcome them back when they have been set free from this demonic oppression.

Remember that term sexual immorality has more than one meaning in the Scriptures. In addition to describing an actual sin of the flesh, it can be used as a symbol for idolatry. Here it has a powerful connection to the churches tendency to get into the idolatrous acts of worshipping the creation rather than the creator (see the book of Hosea). As we continue to read the letter to this church, the Lord makes it clear that this is not the end of the story. The Lord makes a promise. As you consider this wonderful promise in the passage below, begin to do some self-examination. Every person and every church has a little of this controlling spirit inside. The need to have control is at the root of this spirit, and this has to be purged from the church if it is ever to rise to the level of the Lord's calling. Remember: Jesus is Lord! Amen?

Now to you I say, and to the rest in Thyatira, as many as do not have this doctrine, who have not known the depths of Satan, as they say, I will put on you no other burden. But hold fast what you have till I come. And he who overcomes, and keeps My works until the end, to him I will give power over the nations. (Revelation 2:24-26)

I believe this verse contains the central prophetic word and promise for the church in South Korea during this new era. The church is being called and anointed to have power over the nations (spiritually). In other words, this is a call for the church in this nation to reach other nations for the Lord. This is a huge calling and many are far from ready for it. This is the time for the church to get prepared and stay ready for a move of God which is about to break forth. I can still see the number eight hovering over South Korea. Where do you see it?

Then I was given a vision of the fires of the end-time harvest bursting forth from South Korea and spreading like wildfire throughout the world at the end of the age. To accomplish this, the Lord is saying that some preparations need to be made. The body of Christ in South Korea and anywhere else in the world must: 1) hold fast to the true doctrine of Jesus; 2) allow themselves be led by the Holy Spirit; and 3) they need to do all this while they are casting out the spirit of Jezebel. We must remember that time is short and the Lord's return is imminent. We cannot wait any longer. We must begin the work now! Amen?

As I continued in this vision over the South Korean peninsula, I saw very large spiritual hands extending down from Heaven. Each of the hands was distributing food on trays. This speaks of the Lord's great provisions being made ready and available during this season of revival. Some of the food looked like French fries, and I marveled that the Lord would be giving fried food to the people. I was quickly corrected and told that this was manna from heaven. The Lord said this was a fulfillment of the promise given in Revelation 2:17,

He who has an ear, let him hear what the Spirit says to the churches. To him who overcomes, I will give hidden manna to eat. And I will give him a white stone, and on the stone a new name written which no one knows except him who receives it.

As I watched, many true believers were grasping large amounts of manna and placing it on their own plates. As this was happening, I noticed that the amount coming from heaven was not diminished. This spoke to me of the great abundance of provision that the Lord is offering to those who are willing to stand for Him in this time of spiritual warfare. Great grace is coming upon those who know the dangers and yet step out to fight in faith. They are given a special secret knowledge. The secret is that in the end those who are with Christ will overcome. Good news! We win! The victory is ours because we belong to the Victor. Amen and Hallelujah! Remember the lessons of Paul in Ephesians Chapter six:

Finally, my brethren, be strong in the Lord and in the power of His might. Put on the whole armor of God, that you may be able to stand against the wiles of the devil. For we do not wrestle against flesh and blood, but against principalities against powers, against the rulers of the darkness of this age, against spiritual host of wickedness in the heavenly places. Therefore take up the whole armor of God, that you may be able to withstand: in the evil day, and having done all, to stand.
Ephesians 6:10-13

Some of the key scriptures for this time are in the two letters of Peter, the 3 letters of John, and the book of Jude. During times of great warfare and persecution remember 1 Peter 4:12-13, *"Beloved, do not think it strange concerning the fiery trials which try you, as if some strange thing happened to you; but rejoice to the extent you partake of Christ's sufferings, that when His glory is revealed, you may also be glad with exceeding joy.""* We need to get our eyes off of our worries and troubles, and get them fixed back on Jesus. We need to forget what is behind and look ahead to the victory celebration at the end of the age.

The Lord wants you to know that trials will come. You can be certain of that. The enemy wants to stop you and block your destiny. However, the Lord is calling you to be diligent in watching to make certain that the enemy does not strike your church from within. One of the nine principles of war is security. Don't let the enemy get into the camp. You wind up shooting each other in the battle against the enemy. This is one of the enemy's key strategies.

The enemy even found one person in Jesus' camp who had a character defect and was especially susceptible to demonic oppression. That disciple was named, Judas. Jesus had already prophesied this. He said that it had to happen, but woe to the one through whom it comes. Don't let this be you! Trust me! You do not want even one of the "woes" coming in the last days. Be especially aware of the Jezebel spirit. This spirit always comes against the pastor, the pastor's spouse, the elders, and the prophets.

Don't get caught up in grumbling, gossiping, or rebelling against God's anointed leaders. Learn from what happened to Korah and his followers. Never forget what the Lord decreed in 1 Chronicles 16:22, and Psalm 105:15, *"Do not touch my anointed ones, and do my prophets no harm.*" This is exactly what the Jezebel spirit does. She attacks the very people God decreed should never be touched or harmed. You don't want the results of this sin. Always remember that this wicked spirit will lead you to attack those who are anointed leaders, especially pastors and prophets.

It will also tempt you to judge and attack one another. This is a very vicious and destructive spirit. Paul spoke of it and the effects of leaving it unchecked in Galatians 5:15 (NIV), "*If you keep on biting and devouring each other, watch out or you will be destroyed by each other.*" Don't let it happen to you! Always remember the key teachings in the Word of God. One very important one is found in Proverbs 18:21, "*Death and life are in the power of the tongue, and those who love it will eat its fruit.*" You don't want this fruit. Listen carefully to what Peter teaches about it in 2 Peter 2:11, "*angels who are greater in power and might do not bring reviling accusations against them before the Lord.*"

Support your Pastor and God's anointed leaders who serve with Him and minister in His name. Flee from anyone who brings accusations and grumbling against God's anointed leaders. Don't get caught up in a rebellion like Korah and his followers did in the days of Moses. The ground literally opened up and swallowed them alive. Those offering unauthorized fire were destroyed by the fire of God. This must not be allowed to exist in the church at the end of the age.

Why is this so wrong? Why does God abhor it? When we accuse other believers, we are standing in agreement with the enemy. As we continue, we will find ourselves doing his work. Pray continually in the words of Psalm 19:14, "*Let the words of my mouth and the meditation of my heart be acceptable in Your sight, O Lord, my strength and my Redeemer.*" To accomplish this great destiny the Lord has placed before you, you must stand in unity with one another, with Christ and against the devil. As you study the passage below, take very seriously these lessons. The word teaches that one day we will be held accountable for every word which proceeds from our mouths. In Matthew 12: 36-37 Jesus said, "*But I say to you that for every idle word men may speak, they will give account of it in the day of judgment. For by your words you will be justified, and by your words you will be condemned.*" As people in the South used to say: "Watch your mouth!"

> *You therefore, beloved, since you know beforehand, beware lest you also fall from your own steadfastness, being led away with the error of the wicked; but grow in the grace of our Lord and Savior Jesus Christ. To Him be the glory both now and forever. Amen.* (2 Peter 3:17-18)

I have found that many people around the world have made a commitment to be in daily intercessory prayer for both South Korea and Israel. May all who have received the call to intercessory prayer for all the nations be encouraged by these prophetic revelations from the Lord! May your commitment to be in prayer for the end-time harvest be strengthened and increased! May you receive hidden manna as you hold fast to what the Lord has given you! Amen!

(End of vision report)

OTHER BOOKS BY THIS AUTHOR

"A Warrior's Guide to the Seven Spirits of God"–Part 1: Basic Training, by James A. Durham, Copyright © James A. Durham, printed by Xulon Press, August 2011.

"A Warrior's Guide to the Seven Spirits of God"–Part 2: Advanced Individual Training, by James A. Durham, Copyright © James A. Durham, printed by Xulon Press, August 2011.

"Beyond the Ancient Door" – Free to Move About the Heavens, by James A. Durham, Copyright © James A. Durham, printed by Xulon Press, April 2012.

"Restoring Foundations for Intercessor Warriors" by James A. Durham, Copyright © James A. Durham, printed by Xulon Press, May 2012.

"Gatekeepers Arise!" by James A. Durham, Copyright © James A. Durham, printed by Xulon Press, February 2013

"Seven Levels of Glory" by James A. Durham, Copyright © James A. Durham, printed by Xulon Press, June 2013

"100 Days in Heaven" by James A. Durham, Copyright © James A. Durham, printed by Xulon Press, August 2013

"Keys to Open Heaven" by James A. Durham, Copyright © James A. Durham, printed by Xulon Press, November 2014

"Appointed Times" – The Signs and Seasons of Yeshua, by James A. Durham, Copyright © James A. Durham, printed by Xulon Press, December 2014

These Books plus teaching CDs and DVDs are available online at:

www.highercallingministriesintl.com

CPSIA information can be obtained at www.ICGtesting.com
Printed in the USA
LVOW04s2242270815

451876LV00013B/210/P